secrets to
spiritual
SUCCESS

building blocks and
disciplines for living
the Christian life

GREG LAURIE

ALLEN
DAVID
BOOKS

KERYGMA
PUBLISHING   Dana Point, California

secrets to
spiritual
SUCCESS

ISBN 0-977103-0-0
Printed in United States of America

Published by: Kerygma Publishing–Dana Point, California
Coordination: FM Management, Ltd.
Cover design: Christopher Laurie
Editor: Karla Pedrow
Interior Design, Production: Highgate Cross+Cathey, Ltd.

Spur One Another On

*And let us consider how we may spur one
another on toward love and good deeds.*
HEBREWS 10:24 NIV

Do you have a friend who needs your
encouragement? One who needs a real
boost? Ask yourself, "How can I spur
her on?" "What can I say that will make
a difference?" Can you write her a note
of encouragement? Speak words of faith
regarding her situation? Love spurs us on, and
words of kindness from a friend do the same.
Take time to build up your friend in love.

Glory Forever and Ever

*To him who loves us and has freed us
from our sins by his blood, and has made
us to be a kingdom and priests to serve
his God and Father—to him be glory
and power for ever and ever! Amen.*

REVELATION 1:5–6 NIV

Oh, how the love of God propels us to praise!
His everlasting love has saved us, freed us,
and made us His heirs, His children, His own.
There's no other place we can go to receive
such unconditional love. May we continue to
worship Him from now until eternity, offering
praise and glory for this spectacular love!

If you look up into His face and say, "Yes, Lord, whatever it costs," at that moment He'll flood your life with His presence and power. – Alan Redpath

Contents

Introduction
The Choice **Is Yours**

Many of life's failures are people who did not realize how close they were to success when they gave up. — Thomas Edison

L uke 5 tells the familiar story of a time in which Peter and his fishing partners, James and John, went fishing and caught nothing. It is a story of both failure and success in the life of Peter, a man we can all relate to quite easily. The element that turned his failure into success is really quite simple. He had fished all night and caught nothing, but when Jesus came on board his little boat, things took a dramatic turn. As Jesus gave directives to Peter that he followed (though somewhat reluctantly at first), his efforts met with success. I should point out, however, that Peter only had partial success, because he was only partially obedient.

Peter's problem up to this point, which had caused him to have empty nets, was that he was engaged in undirected service. In other words, God had not told him to do what he was doing. Thus, there was no lasting fruit. There were no great results. There was no success because of what he was doing. He was needlessly spinning his wheels, and the results were that he had toiled all night and caught nothing.

Like Peter, maybe you know what it's like to undertake something for God, only to end up failing. Hopefully, the principles we'll be looking at together in the pages ahead will help you discover where you went wrong.

Some of us are a little dense, and instead of pausing to reevaluate, we keep plowing ahead, and we dig ourselves in deeper. How often we have begun a work for God that bears no fruit, because we have not really been directed by Him. How often we have entered into a business deal or a relationship that is a disaster, because we failed to consult with the Lord. If we are smart, we will fail forward—which means that we will learn from the mistakes we have made and hopefully not make them again.

As he looked back at what went wrong, Peter could quickly see he was outside of the will of God. He was not being directed by God. And when he finally was, his partial obedience of Jesus' command brought partial success. If he would have thrown out all the nets, he would have caught all the fish. But because he doubted the Lord, he only threw out one net. That was unfortunate.

And I believe many times in our lives, we miss what God wants to do, because we don't take the first step. If you want God to tell you His agenda for your life for the next month or the next year, you're not going to get it. God leads us one step at a time. He wants you to obey Him and take the step He has already shown you. Many times we don't see what God wants to do in our lives, because we say, "That isn't important. I don't want to do that." So we end up missing out. God wants to do something great in your life. He wants to do a miracle, but you have to obey.

If we live our live God's way and in God's timing, our nets will be breaking, just as Peter's net was, because it is directed service. How often we waste days, months, years, or even a lifetime pursuing things that are not the will of God for us.

You can (and will) succeed if you simply yield to Him and let Him onto your boat—or into your life—and let Him be in control. It makes all the difference in the world.

1 Learn to **Love It**

Always bear in mind that your own resolution to succeed is more important than any one thing. — Abraham Lincoln

S piritual success. It's something we all want as Christians. Sadly, we all know people who have been spiritual failures, and perhaps we may even regard ourselves as such. While some have grown leaps and bounds spiritually, others have not grown at all. While some have done great things for God and His kingdom, others have done nothing.

Why is it that it seems as though Christianity works for some and not for others? "I've tried Christianity," some people say, "but it didn't work for me." Please know this: Christianity is not a product that works for some, but not others. Plain and simple, Christianity is Christ. And He can and will work in any life truly dedicated to Him.

So why is it that some succeed while others fail? That is what this book is about. We have a choice in the matter of living a life that is spiritually barren or blessed by God, a life of disappointing failure or genuine success. The same principle of what the Lord said to Israel applies to us today:

> "Today I have given you the choice between life and death, between blessings and curses. I call on heaven and earth to witness the choice you make. Oh, that you would choose life, that you and your descendants might live! Choose to love the Lord your God and to obey him and commit yourself to him, for he is your life." (Deut. 30:19–20 NLT)

I am not suggesting that living the Christian life is merely human effort, because Scripture teaches, "It is God who works in you both to will and to do for His good pleasure" (Phil. 2:13). But at the same time, I understand that clearly there are some things only *God* can do and some things only *you* and *I* can do. For instance, only God can save a person. Only God can forgive and forget our sins. Only God can change the human heart. But only you and I can believe. Only *you* and *I* can repent. Only *you* and *I* can follow. God will not do those things for us, because He has given us a free will to choose.

Most of us are well aware of the things we *should not* do as Christians. So let's focus on what we *should do.* After all, the best defense is a good offense, as the saying goes.

The Place to Start

To know spiritual success as a follower of Jesus Christ, there are some things that must be a part of your life on a regular, even daily, basis. These are nonnegotiables. They are not for some and not for others. They are for everyone. They are disciplines of the Christian life.

Now "discipline" is a not a word we particularly like. It isn't necessarily a popular word in the twenty-first century, because we live in an instant society. We are always looking for ways to do things faster and easier.

I recently read about a pill that is being developed that supposedly enables those who take it to lose weight. Immediately, the idea of something like that appeals to me, because I don't have to change my diet, and I don't have to exercise. I can reach a desired result without a lot of effort. (That is why I wrote a book called *"I'm Going On a Diet Tomorrow" [And Other Lies We Tell Ourselves]: How to Effectively Resist Temptation.)*

But that is just typical of the quick-fix mentality in our culture today. We don't want to discipline ourselves or wait for anything. We are looking for the magic pill or bullet. Remember something called mail? There was a time when we actually wrote letters, tucked them into envelopes, slapped a stamp on them, and patiently waited for them to reach their destinations. Now we call it "snail mail." Then technology amazed us again with something called a fax machine. How impressive that was to send something by fax, because it was much quicker than the mail. But in time even that seemed slow and cumbersome. Then we came out with e-mail. Now, even e-mail seems slow. So we have instant messaging. We no longer have to wait for the evening news to catch up on the day's events. We can go to the Web or turn to one of the twenty-four-hour news channels.

Only God can change the human heart.

So when it comes to our spiritual lives, we expect instant spirituality. We want it all, and we want it now. Yet the Bible speaks in terms of slowing down, taking root spiritually, studying, denying oneself, and obeying. In other words, discipline.

In fact, the very word "disciple" comes from the root word "discipline." So if you want to grow and experience success as a Christian, then you must learn discipline.

The Parable of the Soils

In Mark 4, Jesus told a story called the Parable of the Sower (that I believe could more accurately be called the Parable of the Soils) about someone who went out to sow seed. As he scattered his seed, some of it fell on the roadside, where the birds came and ate it. Some of the seed fell on ground that was embedded with rocks, and it began to shoot up rather quickly. But because it could not establish roots, it withered in the searing sun. Some seed also fell on ground that was embedded with weeds, and it choked out and impaired the progress of the plant, so it slowly but surely died. Lastly, some seed fell on good ground—receptive soil—and the seed produced fruit.

> *When it comes to our spiritual lives, we expect instant spirituality.*

Jesus then interpreted the parable. He said the seed is the Word of God, and the soil represents the human heart. The seed by the roadside represents people who hear the Word of God, but Satan comes immediately and takes away the Word that was sown in their hearts. This speaks of people who hear the gospel message, but never really respond. It has no effect whatsoever.

The second type of soil is a little bit different. It represents people who hear the Word of God and appear to respond appropriately. There is even some evidence of growth, but then they wither away, because they never became fully rooted. They experience the emotion of the moment and the excitement of it all, perhaps because they responded on impulse or because a friend did, but then they fall away.

The third type of soil represents those who hear God's Word and appear to respond to it, but as time passes, the cares of this life and the love of other things choke it out, and they no longer bear spiritual fruit.

This brings us to the last type of soil: "But these are the ones sown on good ground, those who hear the word, accept it, and bear fruit: some thirtyfold, some sixty, and some a hundred" (v. 20). That is what it is all about—being a fruitful Christian, a growing Christian. In fact, one of the primary reasons we are on this earth is to glorify God and to produce spiritual fruit. Jesus said, "You did not choose Me, but I chose you and appointed you that you should go and bear fruit, and that your fruit should remain, that whatever you ask the Father in My name He may give you" (John 15:16). So how are you doing with this assignment? Are you bearing fruit? Tragically, many believers have not grown at all. They are in a state of arrested development. Sadly, many churches today are full of people who are spiritually weak, immature, undiscerning, and fragile. There is simply no excuse for that.

It is one thing to be a brand-new believer. But if you have known the Lord for awhile, then you should be growing strong, bearing fruit, and experiencing spiritual success. As the author of Hebrews tells us, "So let us stop going over the basics of Christianity again and again. Let us go on instead and become mature in our understanding. Surely we don't need to start all over again with the importance of turning away from evil deeds and placing our faith in God" (6:1 NLT).

The First Secret

Are you satisfied with where you are in your spiritual life? Or have you been more of a failure spiritually than a success? If you want to be a success, then read on. We are about to take a look at the first secret to spiritual success. We find it in Joshua 1:8:

"This Book of the Law shall not depart from your mouth, but you shall meditate in it day and night, that you may observe to do according to all that is written in it. For then you will make your way prosperous, and then you will have good success."

Secret number one: If you want to be a successful Christian, then you must read, study, and love God's Word.

> ### A successful Christian will always be a Bible-studying Christian.

Many years ago, when the young Billy Sunday became a Christian, an older believer gave him some advice that he never forgot. He told him, "William, there are three simple rules I wish you'd practice. If you do, no one will ever write 'backslider' after your name. Take fifteen minutes each day to let God talk to you, allow fifteen minutes to talk to Him, and then spend fifteen minutes telling others about the Savior." Billy Sunday faithfully followed that advice and ultimately became a powerful evangelist whom God used to bring thousands of people into His kingdom.

That is good advice and a good place to begin. So let's look at the first principle: letting God talk to us. How does God speak to us today? First and foremost, He speaks through His Word.

A successful Christian will always be a Bible-studying Christian. The psalmist wrote, "See how I love your commandments, Lord. Give back my life because of your unfailing love. All your words are true; all your just laws will stand forever" (Ps. 119:159–160 NLT). A fruitful believer always will be a lover of God's Word. There is no getting around this. It's Spiritual Success 101.

The Relevance of God's Word

I can still remember the first time I started reading this incredible Book called the Bible. I also remember trying it hide it—not in my heart, but in the bushes. I had been a Christian only one day when someone who had been at the Bible study where I had accepted Christ walked up to me on my high school campus and said, "Brother Greg! I have something for you!" First off, I slightly cringed at him addressing me as "brother," but I did a double take when he pulled out a very large, very thick Bible. To add insult to injury, at least in my mind at that point, the Bible had a cross made of Popsicle sticks glued onto the cover. He told me that if I was going to follow Christ, I needed to start reading the Scripture—and he plopped it into my reluctantly outstretched hand.

Understand, I was in sort of an awkward time in which I hadn't fully acclimated to the Christian life. All of my friends were unbelievers still. So I was in a type of spiritual no man's land, if you will.

I took the very large Bible and sheepishly thanked him. Then I thought, "What am I going to do with this? I can't walk around my high school actually carrying a Bible!" So I shoved it in the pocket of the coat I was wearing, actually ripping my pocket to get the Bible inside and concealed. I didn't want anyone to see what I had. Then I went over to my friend's house where we would often go during lunch, because he lived close to the campus. As I was making my way there, I thought, "I can't go in with a Bible! My friends don't even know I've become a Christian!" So I looked around to see if anyone was watching, and then I took my Bible and hid it in the bushes in front of the house. (So much for being a bold witness for Christ!) Then I casually walked in. One of my friends said, "Greg what have you been doing lately? We haven't seen you around."

"Nothing."

"Where you been?"

My heart was beating faster, and I mumbled, "Nowhere."

Though I knew I should tell these guys about what Christ had done for me, I was simply unwilling to do so. There was a palpable tension in the room. We all knew it. I sensed the Holy Spirit nudging me to tell them, and I was not responding.

As we were sitting there uncomfortably, the front door suddenly opened. My friend's mother walked in. In her hands was *my Bible* with the Popsicle-stick cover!

Then she asked the dreaded question: "Who does this belong to?"

Every eye in the room went to me. Somehow they knew there was some sort of connection between that very large Bible and me.

"That's mine," I replied, nonchalantly.

"Greg, what is that?" asked one of my friends.

"It's a Bible."

"It's a *what*?"

"It's a … ahem … a Bible."

"A *what*?"

"It's a Bible. *A Bible!*" I shouted.

He said, mocking, "Oh, Laurie, are we going to be a good little Christians now and follow Jesus Christ?"

I said, "No. We are going to hit you in the mouth right now. That is what we are going to do." (I hadn't read 1 Corinthians 13 and learned about being patient and kind yet.) I retrieved my Bible and looked around the room. And I realized, after a little bit of ridicule, that if I was going to be a true follower of Jesus, then it would create tension with these people who did not want to walk with God. It also made me more determined to know what the Bible said.

So I began reading the Bible and discovered how relevant it was. I was a seventeen-year-old kid, yet it spoke to my life in every way. It still speaks to me today, and I'm certain it will in the years ahead as well.

Just Read the Directions

The Bible is God's word to us. It is the user's manual we have been looking for in life, showing us who God is and how to know Him and His will. Yet many people never crack it open.

> *Everything we need to know about God is taught in the Bible.*

They don't realize what they are missing, like one young man I heard about who was graduating from college and hoped his father would give him a new car. He had even decided on the one he wanted and told his father about it. But when graduation day came, he was shocked when his father did not hand him the keys to a new car, but a brand-new Bible instead. Outraged, the young man turned and walked away, leaving his father holding the Bible. He never spoke to him again. Some years later, his father died. When he went to his father's house to help get his affairs in order, he noticed the Bible his father had given him, sitting on a shelf. He picked it up and opened it for the first time. Much to his surprise, he found an envelope tucked inside with his name written on it. Inside was a cashier's check in the exact amount of the car, issued on the day of his graduation.

His father *had* given him the car, but he had to open the
Bible to find out. He never realized what his father had
done for him, because he didn't open his Bible.

As sad as this story is, we essentially do the same thing
when we never open this Book our Heavenly Father has
given to us. And there is something far more valuable than
a cashier's check inside. In it are the very words of life, the
truth about how to get to heaven, and the very words of God
to us. What could be more valuable than that?

But many of us, myself included, would rather try out
something first and read the directions later. We usually
end up doing the first thing the user's manual tells us not to
do. Maybe this is why so many products today have warning labels on them. Some are helpful. Still others seem a
little ridiculous, like this label on a cardboard sun shade
for windshields: "Warning: Do not drive with sun shield
in place." This warning is found on instructions for a hair
dryer: "Do not use while sleeping." The warning on an elec-
tric rotary tool reads, "This product is not intended for use
as a dental drill!" A warning for children's cough medicine
advises, "Do not drive or operate machinery." This warning
was found on a child-sized Superman costume: "Wearing of
this garment does not enable you to fly."

Think of all those people who try to dry their hair while
they're sleeping, drive their car with the sun shield still in
place, or fly because they have a giant "S" on their chest. If
only they would read the directions and warning labels first!
But the same is true of life, and the Bible gives us directions
and warnings to guide us and protect us. We are reminded
in 2 Timothy,

> All Scripture is inspired by God and is useful to teach
> us what is true and to make us realize what is wrong

in our lives. It straightens us out and teaches us to do what is right. It is God's way of preparing us in every way, fully equipped for every good thing God wants us to do. (3:16–17 NLT)

The Word of God is also alive. Hebrews 4:12 says, "For the word of God is full of living power. It is sharper than the sharpest knife, cutting deep into our innermost thoughts and desires. It exposes us for what we really are" (NLT). The Bible reveals who we really are, and that may be one of the reasons some people don't like to read it. They don't like what it says about them. They don't like its revealing light shining into their lives. The Bible tells the truth. As Martin Luther said, "The Bible is alive. It speaks to me. It has feet. It runs after me."

> *Churches today are full of people who are spiritually weak.*

Success or failure in the Christian life depends on how much of the Bible we get into our hearts and minds on a daily basis—and on how obedient we are to it. If we neglect the study of Scripture, our spiritual life will ultimately unravel, because everything we need to know about God is taught in the Bible. Show me a Christian who is failing, someone who is backsliding and who is not growing spiritually, and I will show you someone who is not spending time in God's Word. We neglect this at our own peril.

You Need to Eat

A hungry person is a healthy person. One of the ways physician knows whether a person is healthy is by the patient's appetite. When there isn't any appetite, it usually means something is wrong. In the same way, some Christians don't have an appetite for the Word of God. And if that is the case, something is wrong spiritually. In 1 Peter, we are urged to, "Like newborn babies, crave pure spiritual milk, so that by it you may grow up in your salvation" (2:2 NIV).

You know the feeling when you haven't eaten for awhile. Your mood turns sour, you feel tired, listless, and you may even get a headache. You might even think you're getting sick. But what a difference a good meal can make. It can revive you.

> *Christianity is not a product that works for some, but not others.*

The same is true of the study of God's Word. The prophet Jeremiah wrote, "When your words came, I ate them; they were my joy and my heart's delight, for I bear your name, O Lord God Almighty" (15:16 NIV). Sometimes in your spiritual life, you might find yourself asking, "What is wrong with me? Why am I so grumpy? Why do I find myself short-tempered? Why do I feel weak spiritually?" It may be because there is a deficiency of the Word of God in your life. It is not enough to just go hear a message in church. It is not enough to even hear a Bible teaching on a radio or television broadcast or even to read a good Christian book. Nothing takes the place of personal Bible study. And if you want to be a successful Christian, then you must be a Christian who reads and studies and loves the Word of God.

The Final Authority

This is why I am alarmed by a trend in churches today of drifting away from the Bible. It is not neglected altogether;

perhaps it is quoted or referenced on a video screen. But many people are no longer bringing their Bibles to church. And when the Bible is used, it is to support the topic of the day when, in fact, it should be the other way around. The text should define the message, rather than the message defining the text. I believe that all of the Scripture is inspired by God, from Genesis to Revelation—chapter by chapter, verse by verse, line upon line, and precept upon precept. I believe in allowing the Bible to unfold, in its context, to reveal the mind and heart of God. In doing so, we will discover the "whole counsel of God" (see Acts 20:27). The prophet Hosea's cry is still relevant for a number of Christians today: " 'My people are destroyed for lack of knowledge' " (4:6). Today, many believers are failing in the spiritual life, falling into sin, and falling prey to false teachings, because they never have developed the vital discipline of studying God's Word on a regular basis.

The Bible tells us that God has given us His Word, along with people to teach it, so "that we should no longer be children, tossed to and fro and carried about with every wind of doctrine, by the trickery of men, in the cunning craftiness of deceitful plotting, but, speaking the truth in love, may grow up in all things into Him who is the head—Christ" (Eph. 4:14–15).

The best way to spot a counterfeit is to know the genuine. I once was talking with a law enforcement officer about a counterfeit ring that had been recently exposed. When I asked him how authentic the money looked, he told me that he could not tell the difference. However, bank tellers could, because they constantly handle money. The same principle applies for living a successful Christian life: we must be familiar with the genuine Word of God. Jesus said,

"If you abide in My word, you are My disciples indeed" (John 8:31).

We need to learn how to think biblically. And in so doing, we will develop a Christian worldview. This means that we look at our culture, our questions, and our challenges through the lens of Scripture. The Bible is our foundation, and it is our final authority.

> *God is not out to ruin your life.*
> *He wants it to be fulfilled.*

It's Perfect

Now let's see what the Word of God has to say about itself and its benefits. The phrase "the law of the Lord" was a Hebrew term used to define Scripture:

> The law of the Lord is perfect, converting the soul; the testimony of the Lord is sure, making wise the simple; the statutes of the Lord are right, rejoicing the heart; the commandment of the Lord is pure, enlightening the eyes; the fear of the Lord is clean, enduring forever; the judgments of the Lord are true and righteous altogether. More to be desired are they than gold, yea, than much fine gold; sweeter also than honey and the honeycomb. Moreover by them Your servant is warned, and in keeping them there is great reward. (Ps. 19:7–11)

First, we discover "the law of the Lord is perfect" (v. 7). This is in direct contrast to the flawed, imperfect reasonings of humanity. As society changes, we don't need to flow with the winds of change. We can stand on the firm foundation of God's Word.

Things go in and out of style, after all. Consider how dated an old yearbook is. We look at our hair back then and ask, "What was I thinking?" And with access to instant news on the Internet and twenty-four-hour news channels, even the morning newspaper can be dated. But God's Word is always current; it's as fresh as the morning dew. Scripture tells us that "His mercies are new every morning" (Lam. 3:23). God's Word is perfect, whole, complete, and sufficient. There is nothing we need to add to it or take away from it. When 2 Timothy 3:16 tells us that "all Scripture is given by inspiration of God," it literally means, "all Scripture is *breathed* by God."

This means that the Bible is God's infallible Word. The original autographs, the first copies, were without error. There were no mistakes or contradictions. Even with the discovery of the Dead Sea Scrolls, where an older version of some of the writings was discovered, they were still the same. God's Word is perfect.

God's Word is also sufficient. Everything you need to know about God is found in the Bible. You don't need God's Word plus psychology or God's Word plus philosophy or God's Word plus this or that. God's Word is sufficient for your life.

It Transforms Us

Second, we see from Psalm 19 that the Word of God transforms us: "The law of the Lord is perfect, *converting the soul*" (v. 7, emphasis mine). The word "converting" can be translated, "to revive, to restore, to transform." So when you read God's Word, you are revived, restored, and transformed.

Those who aren't really interested in changing or being transformed probably aren't interested in the Bible or in spiritual success. The Bible is for people who have some sense of desperation about where they are in life. It is for people who don't have the purpose in their lives they wish they had. It is for people who don't want to be controlled by their passions, who don't want to be victims of circumstance, and who wish their relationships were better. It is for people who want direction in life, who want to know how to live, and who want to go to heaven. It is for people who want to know God. The Bible is for people who don't have all the answers and want something better.

> *The best way to spot a counterfeit*
> *is to know the genuine.*

And sometimes, the Bible even stops bullets! In 2001, a Bible saved the life of 16-year-old Kenneth Wallace, whose mother tried to shoot him as he stood outside a Florida church one Sunday morning. But the bullet hit Wallace's Bible and coat instead, and according to Sheriff's Deputy Larry King, "Had his Bible not been there he could have been seriously wounded or killed."[1]

It Gives Wisdom

The Bible will save your life too—not by carrying it, necessarily, but by obeying it. It is not enough to simply read and study God's Word. We must do what it says. James reminds us:

> And remember, it is a message to obey, not just to listen to. If you don't obey, you are only fooling yourself. For if you just listen and don't obey, it is like

looking at your face in a mirror but doing nothing to improve your appearance. You see yourself, walk away, and forget what you look like. But if you keep looking steadily into God's perfect law—the law that sets you free—and if you do what it says and don't forget what you heard, then God will bless you for doing it. (James 1:22–25 NLT)

The study of and obedience to God's Word brings us untold benefits, another of which is described in Psalm 19:7: "The testimony of the Lord is sure, making wise the simple." God's Word gives us incredible wisdom. The word "simple" in this verse is translated from a root word in Hebrew that speaks of an open door. It is the idea of a person who has a mind like an open door—everything comes in and goes out. It is the idea of a person who is completely naïve, open to everything, and closed to nothing. This verse tells us the Bible is able to make such a person wise.

This brings us back to the importance of having a biblical worldview. If you believe that human beings are intrinsically good and that no one is evil, then you will have a hard time reconciling human behavior with your ideals. If you believe people are just a product of their environment and if that can be changed, then it will change them, then you will have a lot of questions. But if you accept that people are not basically good, but sinful, as the Scripture teaches, then life will make sense. If you believe that only God can change the human heart, then you will be able to make sense of this world we live in. If you believe that one day Christ will return and true justice will prevail, then you will have hope. That is because you believe the Bible rather than relying on your own opinions, emotions, or what is currently popular or politically correct. We can't let these things dictate how we feel or how we act. We need to think and act biblically and look at the world through a scriptural lens.

Spiritual success takes discipline.

In July 1999, the world was stunned by the tragic news that John F. Kennedy Jr. had been killed in a plane crash, along with his wife and sister-in-law. Kennedy was piloting his private plane to Massachusetts to attend a family wedding in Hyannis Port. But the plane unexpectedly went down off the coast of Martha's Vineyard. Investigators found no apparent mechanical problems with Kennedy's plane. The NTSB cited several factors in the cause of the crash, including spatial disorientation. Kennedy would have been required to trust what his instruments, rather than his physical senses, were telling him. His instincts obviously proved more powerful—and sadly fatal.

If we want to see spiritual success as believers, then we must look to the navigation equipment of God's Word rather than trust our own feelings and ideas. This will guide us safely through the most severe storms and give us the direction we need in life.

It's Right

We also see from Psalm 19 that God's Word is right: "The statutes of the Lord are right, rejoicing the heart" (v. 8). God has presented to us, in the pages of Scripture, the right way to live. Do you want peace, joy, meaning, and purpose in life? The Bible says, " 'Blessed are those who hear the word of God and keep it!' " (Luke 11:28).

Sometimes people wrongly feel that God is out to make

their lives miserable and restrictive with all of His rules. Admittedly, the Bible does tell us not to do certain things as well as urges us in what we should do. But that is for our own good spiritually—and often physically as well. If the Bible tells you to steer clear of a certain activity, relationship, or situation, it is for your spiritual protection. Psalm 84:11 reminds us, "No good thing will the Lord withhold from those who do what is right" (NLT). If it's a good thing, God will not keep you from it. But often what we think of as good is spiritually destructive.

You can lead a happy life without sin, without sex outside of marriage, without drugs or alcohol, and without selfishness. God is not out to ruin your life. He wants it to be fulfilled. And the happiness that He gives doesn't stop when the party is over.

Jesus Christ invites us to an intimate friendship with Him, yet so many people behave as distant relatives. He wants us to get to know Him better. And the way we do that is through the study of His Word. He has said, "'Behold, I have come—in the volume of the book it is written of Me …" (Heb. 10:7). As we read and study it, we will be wise, transformed, and happy people. We will also have the resources to effectively resist temptation.

Spiritual success takes discipline. It means the Bible must be more than a prop; it must be your guide. It means that you need to make time for it each and every day. And it means you must obey what it says. If so, then you will have spiritual success.

Notes

1 "Bible Saves American in Shooting," BBC News, September 3, 2001, http://news.bbc.co.uk/1/hi/world/americas/1523695.stm.

2 Keep the **Line Open**

I have seen many men work without praying, though I have never seen any good come out of it; but I have never seen a man pray without working. —J. Hudson Taylor

Why are some Christians spiritual successes and others are spiritual failures? Why do some run the race of life and win, while others lose? Why do some succeed, while others fail miserably? Because of choices— hundreds that we make every single day. We make our choices, and our choices make us.

It comes back to that word we don't necessarily want to hear, but is an essential to spiritual success—*discipline*. It comes down to disciplines, things we must do to grow and be strong spiritually. To ignore these is to do so at our own peril. You show me a person who is successful at any given thing, and I will show you someone who has learned discipline.

Discipline is a word that many of us wish were not in our vocabulary. But it is a word we need to get comfort- able with—and even more so, embrace. If we are going to succeed as Christians, then we must learn how to discipline ourselves and stay away from anything that would hurt us spiritually. It means cutting loose what could slow us down or impair our performance. In also means embracing what would benefit us spiritually.

Planned Neglect

Someone asked a concert violinist at New York's Carnegie Hall how she became so skilled. "Planned neglect," she answered. She planned to neglect everything that was not related to her goal. The apostle Paul urged "planned neglect" for believers as well: "Run from anything that stimulates youthful lust. Follow anything that makes you want to do right. Pursue faith and love and peace, and enjoy the companionship of those who call on the Lord with pure hearts" (2 Tim. 2:22 NLT).

> *We make our choices, and our choices make us.*

We apply discipline in so many areas of our lives. I have tried to discipline myself to run, but it isn't easy. Apparently, I'm not the only one who feels this way, because 87 percent of Americans who own running shoes don't run. However, I have found that once I get started, running becomes a whole lot easier. And I am always happy afterward that I went running.

Jim Ward, who was one of the best-known triathletes in the world, first began competing in triathlons at age sixty-eight. He was a ten-time world champion in his age group, and at age seventy-seven, had become the oldest athlete to finish the most difficult triathlon of all, the Hawaii Ironman. Just to give you an idea of how difficult this competition is, it involves a 2.4–mile ocean swim, a 112-mile cycling race, and a 26.2-mile run—all in one day. Competitors have seventeen hours to finish the race. Ward had completed more than 150 triathlons, traveling the world to compete. He once told a newspaper journalist that he wanted to complete the Ironman as an octogenarian. Ward was quoted as saying, "I'm not going to quit!" He died at age eighty-three, suffering a heart attack five miles into a long-haul bicycle ride.

Jesus was constantly praying.

I think we can take that same drive, energy, and discipline and apply it to our spiritual lives as well. With discipline and a commitment to run the spiritual race, we all should say, like Jim Ward, "I'm not going to quit!" In the last chapter, we identified the first secret of spiritual success: you must read, study, and love God's Word. Now let's take a look at the second secret to spiritual success.

The Second Secret
To be a successful Christian, you must have a prayer life.

Simply put, prayer is communicating with and listening to God. However, there are many ways to pray, and they are, in reality, different forms of prayer. Paul wrote in Ephesians, "Praying always with all prayer and supplication in the Spirit, being watchful to this end with all perseverance and supplication for all the saints" (6:18). So we see from this verse that we should pray always, with all prayer. … We use the word "prayer" in a general way, but really it speaks of many types of communication with God. We can pray publicly, privately, verbally, or silently. We can pray kneeling, sitting, lying down, or even while we are driving. We can pray with our eyes open or closed. (If you pray while you're driving, I strongly recommend the first option.) You can pray in any position, at any time, anywhere.

Sometimes we think the Lord will perhaps hear our prayers better if they are spoken in a church building, but that is not necessarily true. Daniel prayed from a lion's den. David prayed out in a field. Peter prayed both in and on the water. And Jonah prayed from the belly of a very large fish. Surely God will hear your prayer wherever you are.

The main thing is simply that you pray—and that you are praying always. The word "all" from Ephesians 6:18 speaks of the frequency of prayer: morning, afternoon, and evening.

> *The main thing is simply that you pray.*

Daniel and Nehemiah

The prophet Daniel had a habit of regular prayer. He was in a place of influence in the Babylonian kingdom. Because Daniel was such a man of integrity and godliness, his enemies knew the only way to bring him down was to find something between him and his God. They were aware that, three times each day, Daniel would open up his windows and pray. So they got the king to unwittingly sign a decree that stipulated no one could pray to anyone except him, and thus the king condemned his friend Daniel to a certain death in the lion's den. But what did Daniel do when he heard this decree had been signed? The Bible tells us, "But when Daniel learned that the law had been signed, he went home and knelt down as usual in his upstairs room, with its windows open toward Jerusalem. He prayed three times a day, just as he had always done, giving thanks to his God" (Daniel 6:10 NLT). Daniel "knelt down as usual … just as he had always done." And what was his prayer? Was it one of personal petition, as in, "God, help!"?

That certainly would have been more than understandable. But the text tells us, "He gave thanks to God."

Do your enemies know you pray? Sometimes we feel strange about praying publicly, such as in a restaurant before a meal. Yet 1 Timothy 2:8 tells us, I desire therefore that the men pray everywhere, lifting up holy hands, without wrath and doubting."

The Bible also provides us with the example of Nehemiah, who was a Jew and the cupbearer to Artaxerxes, king of Persia. Being a cupbearer was like being a member of the king's cabinet. It was a position of influence and affluence. You would not only test the king's food and drink before he did, but you also would be a confidant, an advisor. You would have been at the king's side most of the time. Meanwhile, the city of Jerusalem was lying in ruin, and Nehemiah was stirred to do something and use his position for the glory of God. One day, the king noticed Nehemiah looked a bit depressed, so he asked him, "Why are you so sad? You aren't sick, are you? You look like a man with deep troubles" (Neh. 2:2 NLT). I love Nehemiah's answer: "With a prayer to the God of heaven, I replied, 'If it please Your Majesty and if you are pleased with me, your servant, send me to Judah to rebuild the city where my ancestors are buried' " (v. 5 NLT). He didn't have time to say, "Oh king, I will get back to you in ten minutes. I have to pray." He simply breathed "a prayer to the God of heaven." And that is what we can do as well. When you get a call that the principal wants to see you in his office, with a prayer to the God of heaven, you make your way there. When the boss wants to talk to you right away, when someone of importance has summoned you, you can pray right where you are, with your eyes open, without even speaking audibly. "God, give me strength to do the right thing here," or "Lord, I ask for Your wisdom as to what or what not I should now say." It's placing yourself in dependence on your Heavenly Father, who has promised that wisdom if we will just ask (see James 1:5).

When the Bible speaks of "all prayer," it means that everywhere you go, you are conscious of the fact that God is present and is listening to what you have to say.

A Good Reason to Pray

So *why* pray? First and foremost, because Jesus told us to. He left us a model to follow. Throughout the Gospels, we read that Jesus was constantly praying. If you want to read the real "Lord's Prayer," then look at John 17. There Jesus offered a lengthy and beautiful prayer to His Father. We see Him in prayer before He raised Lazarus from the dead, as He spoke first to His Father, "Father, I thank You that You have heard Me. And I know that You always hear Me, but because of the people who are standing by I said this, that they may believe that You sent Me.' Now when He had said these things, He cried with a loud voice, 'Lazarus, come forth!' " (John 11:41–43).

> *We should pray, simply because Jesus told us to.*

When Jesus fed the five thousand, He asked God's blessing on the food (see John 6:11). And mothers brought their children to Him "that He might put His hands on them and pray" (Matt. 19:13).

During the hardest phase of His ministry, Jesus was in constant prayer as well. In the Garden of Gethsemane, He prayed, calling on His Father and saying, "O My Father, if it is possible, let this cup pass from Me; nevertheless, not as

I will, but as You will" (Matt. 26:39). Even on the cross, He prayed, "Father, forgive them, for they do not know what they do" (Luke 23:34) and "My God, My God, why have You forsaken Me?" (Matt. 27:46).

If prayer was such an important part of Jesus' life, then it should be all the more so in ours. In Luke, we read that Jesus told His disciples a parable about a persistent widow "to show them that they should always pray and not give up" (Luke 18:1 NIV). Is there really any better reason? That should be enough to cause us to pray. Still, we have the promise that God answers our prayers. We have the joy of being able to see the hand of God move at our request. Yet we should pray, simply because Jesus told us to. Even if prayer was an extremely difficult task (which it is not), or very unpleasant (which it is not), or even if we never received answers (which we do), we should pray simply because we are commanded to pray.

Just Ask

Second, we should pray because prayer is God's appointed way for us to obtain things. As James 4:2 tells us, "You do not have because you do not ask." You may wonder, "Why it is that I never seem to know the will of God for my life?" *You do not have because you do not ask.* "Why don't I ever have the opportunity to lead people to Christ?" *You do not have because you do not ask.* "Why am I always just scraping by, never having enough?" *You do not have because you do not ask.*

I am not saying that God will answer every one of our prayers in the affirmative, simply because we have taken the time to ask Him, because there are times, for our own good, that the Lord may overrule a request we offer.

But I am saying there are things that God wants to do in your life, and He is simply waiting for you to ask so that He can be glorified in it.

Don't Worry About It

Third, prayer is the way through which God helps us overcome our anxiety and worry. Life is certainly full of troubles and worry. Among other things, we worry about our kids. We worry about our aging parents. We worry about our grandchildren. We worry about our spouse's health. We worry about our own health. We worry about our income. And we worry about the state of our world, especially post–9/11. Yet Philippians says, "Don't worry about anything but pray about everything. Tell God what you need and thank Him for all He has done. If you do this you will experience God's peace which is far more wonderful than the human mind can understand. His peace will guard your hearts and minds as you live in Christ Jesus" (Phil. 4:6–7 NLT). There is so much to worry about, but prayer is the primary way we overcome our anxiety and worry. As it has been said, "If your knees are shaking, kneel on them."

Get Ready

Fourth, prayer is one of the ways in which we make ourselves ready for Christ's return. Jesus said,

> But take heed to yourselves, lest your hearts be weighed down with carousing, drunkenness, and cares of this life, and that Day come on you unexpectedly. For it will come as a snare on all those who dwell on the face of the whole earth. *Watch therefore, and pray* always that you may be counted worthy to escape all these things that will come to pass, and

to stand before the Son of Man." (Luke 21:34–36, emphasis mine)

> *"If your knees are shaking, kneel on them."*

And in speaking of His coming, Jesus said, "But of that day and hour no one knows, not even the angels in heaven, nor the Son, but only the Father. Take heed, watch and pray; for you do not know when the time is" (Mark 13:32–33 NIV).

> *True praying is not overcoming God's reluctance, but laying hold of His willingness.*

So as you can see, prayer is not an option for a believer. If you want God to speak to you, provide for you, help you not to worry, and be ready for Christ's return, then you must pray. To experience spiritual success, along with having a love for God's Word and a desire to study and obey it, we must learn and practice this essential discipline of the Christian life.

Yet we all have had prayers that have gone unanswered— at least in the affirmative, that is. Here is a simple guideline to keep in mind when you are waiting for your prayers to be answered:

If the request is wrong, God says, "No."

If the timing is wrong, God says, "Slow."

If you are wrong, God says, "Grow."

But if the request is right, the timing is right, and you are right, God says, "Go!"

So how can we hear God's "Yes" and "Go!" more often? Are there secrets to answered prayer? Yes and no. On one hand, these are not really secrets, because the Bible is clear in telling us how to approach God and have meaningful communion with Him through prayer. On the other hand, if you don't know these principles, then they indeed could be secrets that will help you unlock the key to a more effective prayer life.

A Pattern for Prayer

These secrets to answered prayer can be found in the Lord's Prayer. Technically, it was not so much the Lord's Prayer as much as it is the disciples' prayer. Or to be more specific, it is a form to follow, a pattern to keep in mind as we approach God:

> Now it came to pass, as He was praying in a certain place, when He ceased, that one of His disciples said to Him, "Lord, teach us to pray, as John also taught his disciples." So He said to them, "When you pray, say: Our Father in heaven, hallowed be Your name. Your kingdom come. Your will be done on earth as it is in heaven. Give us day by day our daily bread. And forgive us our sins, for we also forgive everyone who is indebted to us. And do not lead us into temptation, but deliver us from the evil one."
> (Luke 11:1–4)

Before we utter a word of personal petition, we must first consider whom we are speaking to. He is the Almighty God and yet our Heavenly Father. So we begin our prayer with worship, adoration, and acceptance of His will.

Pray according to God's Will

This brings us to the first secret of answered prayer: If you want your prayer answered in the affirmative, then you must pray according to the will of God. *Your kingdom come. Your will be done …* (v. 2). Jesus modeled this again in Gethsemane as He prayed, "Nevertheless, not as I will, but as You will" (Matt. 26:39). Sometimes God will answer our prayers differently than we expect Him to. This was the case with three men who were hiking through a forest. They came upon a large, raging, violent river, and need-ing to get to the other side, they stopped to pray. The first man prayed, "God please give me the strength to cross this river." Poof! God have him big arms and strong legs, and he was able swim across in about three hours—after nearly drowning twice.

> *Nothing lies outside the reach of prayer*
> *except that which lies outside the will of God.*

Witnessing his friend's ordeal, the second man prayed, "God, please give me the strength and the tools to cross this river." Poof! God gave him strong arms, strong legs, and a rowboat. He was able to row across the river in about an hour—after almost capsizing once.

Seeing what happened to his two friends, the third man prayed, "God, please give me the strength, the tools, and the intelligence to cross the river." Poof! He was turned into a woman. She checked the map, hiked one hundred yards upstream, and walked across the bridge.

We need to know that the primary objective of prayer is to align our will with the will of God. It is only when we do this that we will see more of our prayers answered in the affirmative. True praying is not overcoming God's reluctance, but laying hold of His willingness. Prayer is not getting our will in heaven, but it is getting God's will on Earth. Martin Luther put it this way, "By our praying, we are instructing ourselves more than Him. ..." And 1 John 5:14 promises, "Now this is the confidence that we have in Him, that if we ask anything according to His will, He hears us. And if we know that He hears us, whatever we ask, we know that we have the petitions that we have asked of Him." Nothing lies outside the reach of prayer except that which lies outside the will of God. God only answers the requests that He inspires.

Prayer is surrender—surrender to the will of God and cooperation with that will. It's like being on a boat and throwing the boathook to the shore and pulling. Do you pull the shore to you, or do you pull yourself to the shore? Prayer is not pulling God to your will; it is you being pulled toward His.

Having done that, we come to the place in prayer to mention personal needs: *Give us day by day our daily bread* (v. 3). It is really an amazing thing to consider the fact that this all-knowing, all-powerful, omnipresent, Creator of the universe would take any interest in us personally. As Job observed, "What is man that you make so much of him, that you give him so much attention?" (Job 7:17 NIV). Why would God be concerned about what concerns us? Why would He care about our needs—much less our wants? Why would He commit himself personally to providing our daily bread? Many reasons could be cited, but the most notable is simply that He loves us.

Just as earthly parents love to give gifts to their children, our Heavenly Father loves to give gifts to His. I don't know about you, but I have always had a tendency to spoil my own family, especially my two boys. When I took trips, I would bring back gifts for my oldest son Christopher. They would get bigger and bigger, and finally my wife told me I was overdoing it. I think I have been more careful with my younger son Jonathan, but I still slip every now and then. I can't help it. I love to bless my sons. And in a much greater way, God loves to bless you.

> *The more we contemplate the holiness of God, the more we will see our own sinfulness.*

Confess Your Sins

Now we come to the second secret of answered prayer: If you want your prayer answered in the affirmative, then you must confess your personal sin. *Forgive us our sins ...* (v. 4). Or literally, "Forgive us our trespasses, shortcomings, resentments, what we owe to You, and the wrong we have done."

Some think they don't need forgiveness, but according to Jesus in this, the model prayer, it is something we should be asking for on a regular basis. According to 1 John 1:8, "If we say that we have no sin, we deceive ourselves, and the truth is not in us." And Paul wrote, "I don't mean to say that I have already achieved these things or that I have already reached perfection! ... No, dear brothers and sisters, I am still not all I should be, but I am focusing all my energies on this one thing: Forgetting the past and looking forward to what lies ahead ..." (Phil. 3:12–13 NLT). Those who do not see a constant need for regular cleansing are not spending much time in God's presence, because when we have truly prayed, "Our Father in heaven, hallowed be Your name," we will then pray, "Forgive us our sins."

There is an interesting scene in the book of Isaiah. Isaiah describes a glorious scene of being in God's presence. The angels are worshipping and crying out to the Lord. The singing was so powerful, it shook the temple. Isaiah, as great as a prophet as he was, found himself deeply humbled, and he said, "I am a sinful man and a member of a sinful race" (Isa.6:5 NLT).

The more we contemplate the holiness of God, the more we will see our own sinfulness. It has been said, 'The greater the saint, the greater is the sense of sin and the awareness of sin within." I find it interesting in Paul's writings that he went from being "the least of all the saints" (Eph. 3:8) to the chief of sinners (see 1 Tim. 1:15). Now that is spiritual growth!

> *The person who has known God's forgiveness must forgive others.*

If you have unconfessed sin in your life, then your prayers are going nowhere, really. The psalmist said, "If I regard iniquity in my heart, the Lord will not hear" (Ps. 66:18). The fact is, we don't necessarily even know what sins we may have committed. The Bible speaks of sins of commission and omission. The sin of commission is to do what God does not want you to do. In contrast, a sin of omission is not doing what God wants you to do. Generally, if our hearts are tender toward the Lord, we will know it when we have engaged in a sin of commission and have crossed that line or done something that displeases Him. But the sin of omission is a bit trickier. James tells us, "Remember, it is sin to know what you ought to do and then not do it"

(James 4:17 NLT). This would be one of those times when the Lord would direct you personally to pray more or perhaps share the gospel with someone, and you find yourself refusing. This is why Jesus tells us in the model prayer, the Lord's Prayer, to ask regularly for the forgiveness of our sins.

Why is this important? When we have unconfessed sin in our lives, God does not answer our prayers for the most part. The prophet Isaiah said, "Your iniquities have separated you from your God; and your sins have hidden His face from you, so that He will not hear" (Isa. 59:2). There may be some sin in your past that has remained unjudged and unconfessed. But God cannot forgive the sin you will not confess. There may be some sin you are committing now that you don't think is sin. We would do well to follow the example of David, the psalmist, who prayed, "Search me, O God, and know my heart; try me, and know my anxieties; and see if *there is any* wicked way in me, and lead me in the way everlasting" (Ps. 139:23–24, emphasis mine). So, to the best of your ability, ask the Lord for the forgiveness of sin in your life.

Forgive Others

The third secret of answered prayer is that we must forgive others. "And forgive us our sins, for we also forgive everyone who is indebted to us" (v. 4). This is a very important principle and one that is often missed. This verse isn't saying that God's forgiveness hinges on our forgiveness of others. Rather, our forgiveness of others should hinge on our understanding of God's gracious and generous forgiveness of us. The proof that you and I are forgiven and have accepted God's forgiveness is that we forgive. The person who has known God's forgiveness must forgive others. And in many ways, forgiveness is the key to all healthy, strong, and lasting relationships, because as fatally flawed people, we will sin. We will hurt one another, whether intentionally or unintentionally. Husbands will offend wives, and wives will offend husbands. Parents will hurt their children, and children will hurt their parents. Family members will offend one another. That is why we must learn to forgive. Ephesians 4:32 instructs us to "be kind to each other, tenderhearted, forgiving one another, just as God through Christ has forgiven you" (NLT). And Jesus said, "Therefore if you bring your gift to the altar, and there remember that your brother has something against you, leave your gift there before the altar, and go your way. First be reconciled to your brother, and then come and offer your gift" (Matt. 5:23–24). Is there someone you need to forgive? If you want your prayers answered, then you need to do it.

Stay Out of Temptation's Way

Now let's look at the fourth secret of answered prayer: As much as possible, stay out of the way of temptation. "And do not lead us into temptation, but deliver us from the evil one" (v. 4). I recognize that we cannot completely remove ourselves from temptation. Otherwise, we would have to leave the planet. But this is a prayer that says, "Lord, don't let me be tempted above my capacity to resist." The problem with temptation is that we can often rationalize it. We tell ourselves that whatever it is we're tempted to do is not a sin. But if we could see our own temptations as well as we see the temptations others struggle with, they wouldn't be that hard to identify. We see others give in to temptation and ask, "How could they do that?" Their sin looks so ugly and foolish. Yet we manage to rationalize our own sin. It somehow seems different, even acceptable. It's the classic plank-in-the-eye syndrome:

For with what judgment you judge, you will be judged; and with the measure you use, it will be measured back to you. And why do you look at the speck in your brother's eye, but do not consider the plank in your own eye? Or how can you say to your brother, "Let me remove the speck from your eye"; and look, a plank is in your own eye? (Matt. 7:2–4)

One day, our little house of cards will collapse, and we will see our sin for what it is. Here's a little test to apply when you are not sure whether something is an enticement to evil:

1. *Pray about it, and bring it into the clear light of the presence of God.* Ask yourself, "Should I allow myself to be in this potentially vulnerable situation?" Jesus said, "Watch and pray, lest you enter into temptation" (Matt. 26:41). Often the reason we are not willing to pray about it is because we already know what the answer will be.

2. *Consider how you would react if you saw another Christian doing the same thing.* How would it look to you? A good prayer to lift up to your Heavenly Father at a time like this would be, "Lord, I know my own sinful vulnerabilities, and I ask You to keep me from the power of sin. Help me to make the right choices and avoid anything that would pull me away from you.

Don't Give Up

Now we arrive at the fifth and final secret of answered prayer: Don't give up. Jesus followed up His lesson on how to pray with a parable that illustrates the importance of persistent prayer.

> And He said to them, "Which of you shall have a friend, and go to him at midnight and say to him, 'Friend, lend me three loaves; for a friend of mine has come to me on his journey, and I have nothing to set before him'; and he will answer from within and say, 'Do not trouble me; the door is now shut, and my children are with me in bed; I cannot rise and give to you'? I say to you, though he will not rise and give to him because he is his friend, yet because of his persistence he will rise and give him as many as he needs. (Luke 11:5–8)

Much of our prayer has no power in it,
because there is no heart in it.

Jesus used an example the people of this culture would have been familiar with. In that day, family members generally did not have their own rooms. There would be a common sleeping area for the entire family. So one person getting up in the middle of the night would wake everyone. Yet here comes this neighbor who would not take "no" for an answer. Jesus concluded the parable by saying, "So I say to you, ask, and it will be given to you; seek, and you will find; knock, and it will be opened to you. For everyone who asks receives, and he who seeks finds, and to him who knocks it will be opened" (Luke 11:9–10). Jesus' language is unusually compelling in these verses, as the verbs "ask," "seek," and "knock" indicate an ascending intensity.

The word "ask" implies a request for assistance. We realize our need and ask for help. It implies a certain humble, low-key approach, like gently trying to get the attention of your server in a restaurant.

"Seek" denotes asking, but adds action to it. It is the idea of not just expressing our need, but actually looking around for help. It involves effort.

"Knock" includes asking, in addition to acting and persevering. It is like someone pounding on a closed door.

A few years ago, I was in a coffee shop in New York with my friend and fellow pastor, Mike Finizio. Now Mike is a seasoned New Yorker, while I am a classic Southern Californian. I wanted our waitress to bring me more coffee, so I very politely said to her, "Excuse me, could I get some more coffee?"

She completely ignored me. So I tried again.

"Sorry to bother you. Could I get some more coffee?"

Still no response. I had noticed the way Mike talked to her seemed a little aggressive. It was the New Yorker way, sort of a friendly aggression. He would call out loudly, "Hey! I need some more coffee here!" and she would respond immediately.

So I tried to emulate Mike's technique.

"Hey!" I said, trying to sound like Mike. "Could I get some more coffee here?"

She looked over at me and said, "You shut up!"

There obviously is something in the rhythm of a New Yorker's speech and delivery that I, as a Southern Californian, don't seem to have.

The sequence of the words in these verses is extremely forceful. A literal translation of the text would read, "*Keep on asking,* and it will be given to you. *Keep on seeking,* and you will find it. *Keep on knocking,* and the door will be opened." Jesus is calling us to passionate, persistent prayer. Much of our prayer has no power in it, because there is no heart in it. If we put so little heart into our prayers, then we cannot expect God to put much heart into answering them. God promises that His people will find Him when they search for Him with all their heart (see Jer. 29:13).

So don't give up. Don't stop praying. As one commentator said, "Men may spurn our appeals, reject our message, oppose our arguments, despise our persons—but they are helpless against our prayers."

Get Right (and Stay Right) with God

Do you know how to pray? Is there something hindering your prayers from being answered? Maybe it is unconfessed sin in your life. Maybe it is unforgiveness toward someone who has wronged you. Or, perhaps you are unnecessarily putting yourself in the way of temptation, and you just can't figure out why you are always getting into trouble. Maybe you're not sure whether any of these things I just mentioned are true of you. The best way to be sure you are right with God is to pray, like David, "Search me, O God, and know my heart; test me and know my anxious thoughts. See if there is any offensive way in me, and lead me in the way everlasting" (Ps. 139:23–24 NIV). The first thing you need to do, even before taking the steps to spiritual success I've already mentioned, is to get right with God and confess your sins (see Isa. 59:1).

Then you can begin to take the steps we've reviewed so far: reading, studying, and loving God's Word; and having a consistent prayer life. These are two secrets to spiritual success. And there are more to come.

③ Everybody Needs **Somebody**

When a Christian shuns fellowship with other Christians, the devil smiles. When he stops studying the Bible, the devil laughs. When he stops praying, the devil shouts for joy. —Corrie ten Boom

One Sunday morning, a husband and wife were getting ready to go to church when she noticed he hadn't even begun to get himself ready. She asked him why he wasn't getting ready for church.

"Because I don't want to go," he said.

"Do you have any reasons?" she asked.

"Yes, I have three good ones," he told her. "First, the congregation is cold. Second, no one likes me. And third, I just don't want to go."

"Well, honey, I have three good reasons why you *should* go," his wife replied. "First, the congregation *is* warm. Second, there are a few people there who like you. And third, you are the pastor. So get dressed."

What is your attitude when it comes to attending church? Is your attitude like that of David, the psalmist, who wrote, "I was glad when they said to me, "Let us go into the house of the Lord" (Ps. 122:1)? Or is it more like "I was *sad* … " or even worse, "I was *mad* … "?

The Third Secret

Because you are reading this book, I'm assuming you want to know the secrets of spiritual success. So far, you've learned that if you want to be a successful Christian, then you must read, study, and love God's Word. You have also learned that to be a successful Christian, you must have a regular and consistent prayer life. Now I want to share with you the third secret to spiritual success.

To be a successful Christian, you must be actively involved in the church. When you miss church, you miss out on a lot, because something wonderful and yes, even supernatural, happens when God's people gather together in His name. As I have already pointed out, you can and will benefit from personal Bible study. You can also have a great time worshipping the Lord by yourself. But when you get together to study His Word and to worship and pray with other believers, the Lord manifests His presence in a special way.

> *Neglect of fellowship with other believers is a sure sign of backsliding.*

Now some may say, "I don't need church to get close to God. I can worship Him out in nature or on the golf course. I can worship him as I am surfing or hiking or fishing. I'll even take along my Bible and say a little prayer." It reminds me of the pastor who decided to skip church one Sunday morning. It was a beautiful day, and he wanted to go golfing, so he told his associate pastor that he wasn't feeling well and asked him to preach that day. Then the pastor left town and went to a golf course about eighty miles away to ensure he wouldn't run into anyone from the church.

As the pastor was teeing up, God was watching from heaven, and an angel remarked to Him, "That preacher should be in his church preaching, not out there golfing! It's Sunday morning! Are You going to let him get away with that?"

"No, I won't," God gently replied.

Just then, the pastor hit the ball. It shot straight toward the pin, dropped just short of it, and then rolled up and fell into the hole. It was a 320-yard hole in one!

The angel was astonished. He looked at God and said, "Why did you let him do that?"

God smiled and replied, "Who on earth is he going to tell?"

We miss out on so much when we are not in fellowship with other believers at church. Some people claim that the Bible doesn't command them to go to church and that it was something people invented. But the Bible indeed commands us to be an active part of His Church. Hebrews 10:24–25 tells us, "And let us consider one another in order to stir up love and good works, *not forsaking the assembling of ourselves together,* as is the manner of some, *but exhorting one another,* and so much the more as you see the Day approaching" (emphasis mine). Or, as another translation puts it, "Think of ways to *encourage one another to outbursts of love and good deeds.* And *let us not neglect our meeting together,* as some people do, *but encourage and warn each other,* especially now that the day of his coming back again is drawing near" (NLT, emphasis mine).

The fact is that neglect of fellowship with other believers is a sure sign of backsliding. Studies have shown that if you don't go to church for one month, the odds are almost two to one that you won't go for more than a year. Being in fellowship is proof that you are a child of God. We are told in 1 John 3:14, "If we love our Christian brothers and sisters, it proves that we have passed from death to eternal life. But a person who has no love is still dead" (NLT). And we read in Psalm 133:1, "Behold, how good and how pleasant it is for brethren to dwell together in unity!" A person's failure to go to church is proof there is something wrong with them spiritually. As 1 John 2:19 says, "These people left our churches because they never really belonged with us; otherwise they would have stayed with us. When they left us, it proved that they do not belong with us" (NLT).

> *Some churches are always planning for the future; other churches live in the past.*

I hope that you have discovered the joy and the blessing of being an active part of a body of believers. And I want to share with you some of the wonderful facets of why we should go to church and the spiritual blessings that will come our way as a result. There are many spiritual benefits we receive from gathering to hear God's Word, worship, and serve together. Jesus himself established the church and said "the gates of Hades shall not prevail against it" (Matt. 16:18). It is a place where we refocus, learn, and grow, a place where we can come to God and help others to do the same. It is a place to both receive from God and give back to others. And it is something we all need to be a part of if we want to succeed spiritually.

A healthy church will be a growing church, and where there is no growth, there is a problem. Some churches have parking problems; other churches don't. Some churches have kids running around making a lot of noise; other churches tend to be very quiet. Some churches usually have more expenses than money; other churches don't need to spend much money. Some churches are growing so fast that you don't always know everyone's name; in other churches, everyone has known each other's names for years. Some churches are always planning for the future; other churches live in the past. Some churches evangelize; other churches fossilize.

More than thirty years ago when we started Harvest Christian Fellowship, the church where I pastor, we built on the foundation of God's Word. I was only twenty years old and had been a Christian for three years. I had a heart full of zeal and limited knowledge. I hadn't been to seminary or Bible school, but I had been in intensive Bible study as a result of attending Calvary Chapel of Costa Mesa for three years. Frankly, my training was on the job. But I felt that if I concentrated on the quality, then God, in His timing, would bring the quantity. I had no idea the Bible study I was leading for young people would grow into a church. I tried to get others to take that Bible study over for me, but no one would. So I went to the Book of Acts and read these verses:

> And they continued steadfastly in the apostles' doctrine and fellowship, in the breaking of bread, and in prayers. Then fear came upon every soul, and many wonders and signs were done through the apostles. Now all who believed were together, and had all things in common, and sold their possessions and goods, and divided them among all, as anyone had need. So continuing daily with one accord in the temple, and breaking bread from house to house, they ate their food with gladness and simplicity of heart, praising God and having favor with all the people. And the Lord added to the church daily those who were being saved. (Acts 2:42–47)

I followed the pattern found in this passage, and I can honestly say that I do not regret that. I believe we did it the right way.

The W-E-L-L Church: Worship

The early church described here was so alive, so healthy. What was it about them that "turned the world upside down" (see Acts 17:6)? It was a W-E-L-L church:

W – Worshipping
E – Evangelizing
L – Learning
L – Loving

First, they were a worshipping church: "Praising God and having favor with all the people . . . the Lord added to the church daily those who were being saved (v. 47). These early believers spent time worshipping God. And that is what we ought to do. Jesus said, "For where two or three are gathered together in My name, I am there in the midst of them" (Matt. 18:20). This doesn't mean that God is not omnipresent. But what it does mean is that God shows himself in a special way when His people gather together for worship. There is nothing in this world like it: that special bond we sense, that blessing of God, and that sense of fulfillment as we do what we were created to do. We were made to glorify God. We were wired to worship. Psalm 106:1 says, "Praise the Lord! Oh, give thanks to the Lord, for He is good! For His mercy endures forever." And Colossians 3:17 reminds us, "And whatever you do in word or deed, do all in the name of the Lord Jesus, giving thanks to God the Father through Him."

From Genesis to Revelation, our faith is one of music, worship, and singing. And when we get to heaven, we are going to sing, so you might as well get started now. Revelation 15 tells us, "And I saw what looked like a sea of glass mixed with fire and, standing beside the sea, those who had been victorious over the beast and his image and over the number of his name. They held harps given them by God and sang the song of Moses the servant of God and the song of the Lamb … " (vv. 2–3).

> *Worshipping God with other believers helps us put our lives into perspective.*

Some may argue they don't have a good voice, so they don't want to sing. But neither do hundreds of contestants on *American Idol*, and that doesn't stop them. (Be glad you don't have a panel of judges critiquing your worship!) There are also times when we don't feel like worshipping, yet Hebrews 13:15 tells us, "Therefore by Him let us continually offer the sacrifice of praise to God, that is, the fruit of our lips, giving thanks to His name." Praise and worship can sometimes feel like a sacrifice, because we don't want to do it. That may be because we are depressed or things aren't going well. Or it may be that a hardship or tragedy has happened in your life, and you don't want to thank God. But the Bible doesn't say, "Give thanks to the Lord when you feel good." It says, "Give thanks to the Lord, for He is good!" (Ps. 106:1).

Did you know that your worship is a witness? As verse 47 tells us, "*Praising God* and *having favor* with all the people. And *the Lord added to the church daily those who were being saved*" (emphasis mine). There is a direct connection between worship and witness. We are being watched both inside and outside of the church. The world marvels when a child of God can rejoice when things go horribly. But in the church sitting next to you may be unbelievers who are essentially evaluating everything by what they see around them—not just by what happens up front, but also by the people around them.

When you are worshipping, do you sing out to the Lord? Or, do you sit in silence, or worse, talk with the person next to you? Worship isn't the warm-up act. It is the reason we are there in the first place: to worship through song, giving, listening to God's Word, and even witnessing. Can someone see your heart for God expressed in your praise? When we as Christians worship God as we ought to, it touches unbelievers. David would play his harp for the tormented King Saul (see 1 Sam. 16:23). Worship brought temporary relief to the wicked king. That is one of the reasons we incorporate worship into our large-scale evangelistic events that we call Harvest Crusades, because the world has nothing quite like it. It soothes unbelievers to some degree, at least temporarily. It provides a bridge to the message of the gospel.

> *There is a trend in the church today of moving away from biblical preaching.*

In fact, it was a group of worshipping believers that first got my attention as an unbeliever. I was jaded. I was hard. If someone would have invited me to church, I can pretty much say that I would not have gone. But on my high school campus, there were these outspoken Christians who would openly worship the Lord in their Bible studies on the front lawn at lunchtime. I went to one of their meetings, and as I watched them singing to God, I saw they had something I did not have. It was as though they were having an intimate conversation with God, and indeed they were. I had been to a lot of concerts and listened to countless albums over the years, yet this simple music deeply touched me. It opened up my heart to the message of God's Word. So it is important to be a worshipper. And it is important that our hearts are right, because our worship of God can either draw people in or drive them away.

A classic example is Paul and Silas. They were thrown into a prison for preaching the gospel. By prison, I mean a dark dungeon. There was no ventilation and there were no sanitation facilities. It was a real hellhole. To make matters worse, their backs were ripped open from being whipped, and their feet were in stocks. And what do we read about them? "But at midnight Paul and Silas were praying and singing hymns to God, and the prisoners were listening to them" (Acts 16:25). It had been a long time since anything like that had been heard in this prison, and they were listening carefully.

Then an earthquake hit. Their singing must have brought the house down, literally. The jailer was ready to kill himself, because if one of his prisoners escaped, under Roman law it meant he would be tortured and executed. He was ready to take his own life when Paul and Silas intervened, calling out, "Do yourself no harm, for we are all here." The jailer came to them and asked, "Sirs, what must I do to be saved?" Their worship earned them the right to witness to him, because they praised God in the midst of adversity.

Sometimes in worship, there is little to no thought of God. If that is the case, then we are not really worshipping. Worship is really a form of prayer. And the sad but amazing thing is that we can sing worship songs to God without a single thought of Him while we are doing it. Jesus spoke of this type of detached worship when He quoted the words of Isaiah, " 'These people draw near to Me with their mouth, and honor Me with their lips, but their heart is far from Me. And in vain they worship Me, teaching as doctrines the commandments of men' " (Matt. 15:8–9). As we drone on, we are really thinking, "I'm hungry," or "They need to turn up the air conditioning," or "When will this service be over?"

> *When we isolate ourselves from other*
> *believers, we lose perspective.*

A lot of it comes down to what is happening in our hearts. As the great British preacher C. H. Spurgeon said, "God does not regard our voices, he hears our hearts. And if our hearts do not sing, we have not sung at all." Jesus told the story of the Pharisee and the tax collector who went to pray (or worship):

The Pharisee stood and prayed thus with himself, "God, I thank You that I am not like other men— extortioners, unjust, adulterers, or even as this tax collector. I fast twice a week; I give tithes of all that I possess.' And the tax collector, standing afar off, would not so much as raise his eyes to heaven, but beat his breast, saying, "God, be merciful to me a sinner!" I tell you, this man went down to his house justified rather than the other; for everyone who exalts himself will be humbled, and he who humbles himself will be exalted." (Luke 18:11–14)

Sometimes we sing worship songs, but we do not worship. Sometimes we pray with our lips, but worship doesn't take place. Sometimes we give to the church, but we aren't worshipping. And sometimes we do none of these things, but we are in our deepest worship. That is because the heart of the matter is the matter of the heart.

Worshipping God with other believers helps us put our lives into perspective. We can come to worship God, and our problems can seem so big. This is because we have things out of perspective. That is why David said, "Oh, magnify the Lord with me, and let us exalt His name together" (Ps. 34:3). When we come to God in prayer and in worship, we see things correctly. This is why Jesus taught us to pray, "Our Father in heaven. ... " No matter what we are facing, when we come to God in prayer, the all-powerful, all-knowing God of the universe loves us and is listening to us. As Jesus said, "Do not fear, little flock, for it is your Father's good pleasure to give you the kingdom" (Luke 12:32).

When we isolate ourselves from other believers, we lose perspective. We can get fearful, confused, angry, and even bitter. This was true of the skeptical Thomas, who was not present with the other disciples when the resurrected Jesus appeared among them. When they told him about it, he said, "Unless I see in His hands the print of the nails, and put my finger into the print of the nails, and put my hand into His side, I will not believe" (John 20:25). But the next time they met, Thomas was there. And his faithfulness was rewarded as he saw the risen Lord for himself.

Asaph was grappling with the age-old question of why the ungodly prosper. And then it dawned on him: "When I tried to understand all this, it was oppressive to me till I entered the sanctuary of God; then I understood their final destiny" (Ps. 73:16–17 NIV). In other words, "I didn't understand why things were the way they were until I came into God's presence to study His Word with His people. Then my questions were brought into their proper perspective." Worship affects every aspect of our lives, and when we neglect it, it affects everything about us.

The W-E-L-L Church: Evangelism

Second, the early church was an evangelistic church: "And the Lord added to the church daily those who were being saved" (v. 47). The church is here for the evangelization of the world, because Jesus commanded us, "Go therefore and make disciples of all the nations, baptizing them in the name of the Father and of the Son and of the Holy Spirit, teaching them to observe all things that I have commanded you" (Matt. 28:19–20). Clearly it is our commission. But I believe that evangelism is the overflow of other things taking place in the church. When we are being built up as believers, we will then want to share our faith, because healthy, well-fed Christians will reproduce themselves.

> *The primary way God chooses to reach humanity is through preaching.*

Of course, we must keep these principles in their proper balance. We are not to emphasize one at the expense of the other. This is what concerns me about churches that engage in what is known as niche marketing, where a certain demographic is targeted. These are churches that say, "We're called to minister to Baby Boomers," or, "We are marketing our ministry to Generation Xers." I don't think that is healthy. I think the church is here for everyone. If a certain group of people comes and is ministered to, that is great. But I don't think we should cater primarily to a certain group. We want to be here to minister to the needs of the people who come.

Then there will be churches that say, "Our church is not called to evangelism. We are called to study the Word together. We're not called to outreach. There are other churches called to evangelism." Wrong. Every church is called to evangelism.

Then another church may say, "We are called primarily to evangelism. We're not really into teaching God's people. There are a lot of churches you can go to and learn the Bible, but we are here to reach the unchurched. Therefore, we have seeker-sensitive services in which we speak in a cultural language that people will understand. We're not called to be keepers of the aquarium. We're called to be fishers of men." That is a clever little saying, but if you are the church, then you are called to minister to God's people. And you are called to evangelism. There must be balance. We can't pick and choose what we want to focus on. Otherwise, we are interfering with God's plan and purpose for His church.

The W-E-L-L Church: Learning

Third, the early church was a learning church. This is something vital to understand. God has ordained preaching and teaching. It is fine to listen to Christian radio or watch Christian television and read Christian books—that is, if it is supplemental to the teaching you are already receiving at church or if it is due to extenuating circumstances. But nothing takes the place of getting together with believers and hearing God's Word. There is freshness and immediacy to it. Don't miss out on what God has for you.

To those who are called to preach God's Word, the Bible says,

> Preach the word of God. Be persistent, whether the time is favorable or not. Patiently correct, rebuke, and encourage your people with good teaching. For a time is coming when people will no longer listen to right teaching. They will follow their own desires and will look for teachers who will tell them whatever they want to hear. (2 Tim. 4:2–3 NLT)

Worship affects every aspect of our lives. …

This is important, because there is a trend in the church today of moving away from biblical preaching. Many churches employ drama, skits, videos, music, and even dance. While I love all the tools we can use to bring the gospel to people, I know that nothing can ever take the place of the proclamation of God's Word. In some churches, however, preaching is seen as outdated, something from another time. Some would reject the idea of communicating absolute truth, suggesting that we instead should be asking questions, not necessarily giving answers. I could not disagree more. I am thrilled when people come to church with their questions, and this is indeed the place to find the answers they have been searching for—granted, not all of the answers. That won't happen until we get to heaven. On the other hand, many, if not most, of our questions will be answered from God's Word as we are engaged in fellowship with His people. It is vital to note that the early church, the church that changed the world, had preaching and teaching: "And they continued steadfastly in the apostles' doctrine … " (Acts 2:42). There is no getting around it. Preaching is the main way God reaches the unbeliever and builds up the believer.

After all, Jesus was a preacher of God's Word. The Bible tells us that when He began His ministry, "From that time Jesus began to preach and to say, 'Repent, for the kingdom of heaven is at hand' " (Matt. 4:17). Then He sent His disciples out to preach as well, saying, "And as you go, preach, saying, 'The kingdom of heaven is at hand' " (Matt. 10:7).

There are many ways God could have reached us here on planet Earth. He could have dropped down visual images such as photographs or paintings to describe what He wanted us to know. Certainly God speaks to us to some degree through the testimony of nature. Psalm 19:1 tells us, "The heavens tell of the glory of God. The skies display his marvelous craftsmanship" (NLT). But the primary way God chooses to reach humanity is through preaching. In the Old Testament, God spoke primarily through the preaching of the prophets. Moses, Isaiah, Jeremiah, Elijah, and others fearlessly preached His Word. In the New Testament, God called the apostles and even common, untrained people to preach. Paul's words to Timothy were, "Preach the word!" (2 Timothy 4:2). When Paul was on Mars Hill, he could have used drama. After all, drama originated in Greece. He could have had someone act out his message or set it to music. But instead, he preached. And preaching is God's primary way of reaching lost people. As 1 Corinthians 1:21 tells us, "For since, in the wisdom of God, the world through wisdom did not know God, it pleased God through the foolishness of the *message preached* to save those who believe" (emphasis mine). Music, drama, and the arts all have their place, but they are nowhere near the importance of preaching and teaching the Word of God. Please understand, I have a great love for the arts and the art community. Before I began my ministry, I myself was a graphic designer and am still involved in design. I have the deepest appreciation for a well-written story, a powerful film, or a beautiful song. But as wonderful as all these things are, God has primarily chosen to reach us and teach us through biblical preaching.

What if all the church were just like you? In a sense, it is.

I know this is true not only because the Bible says it, but also from personal experience. I have had the privilege of speaking for more than thirty years at Harvest Christian Fellowship, as well as great stadiums and arenas, and in small settings where we all sat on grass mats. In every location, it was God's Word preached that touched lives.

Trust me when I tell you that the last thing I ever wanted to become was a preacher. When I was in school, I was never involved in public speaking. In fact, I dreaded giving a speech. But the first time I preached, I saw the power of God at work. My life was touched by the teaching and preaching of God's Word, and it still is. I listen to it all the time.

But it is not only strong preaching that we need. We also need strong listening. How often did Jesus say, "He who has ears to hear, let him hear!"? Verse 42 says the early church *"continued steadfastly* in the apostles' doctrine…" (emphasis mine). To "continue steadfastly" speaks of a real passion. They were living in a first-love relationship with Jesus. Theirs was not a casual attitude of someone joining a social club.

There seemed to be a spiritual excitement surrounding what they did. They applied themselves to what was being taught from God's Word.

We need New Testament Christianity.

In the same way, we need to listen not only with our heads, but with our hearts, having an openness to receive God's Word. We must not only want to hear it, but we must also want to apply it. Jesus said, "Whoever hears these sayings of Mine, and does them, I will liken him to a wise man who built his house on the rock: and the rain descended, the floods came, and the winds blew and beat on that house; and it did not fall, for it was founded on the rock" (Matt. 7:24–25). This means that we must give priority not only to listening to biblical teaching, but also to applying what we hear.

What if all the church attended services as faithfully as you do? Would the seats be empty or full? What if all the church worshipped just like you do? Would the congregation fall silent or sing joyfully and loudly to the Lord? What if all the church heard the Word of God with the same attitude you have? Would lives be changed? What if all the church were just like you? In a sense, it is. It is made up of people like you and me. And every one of us either contributes to its strength and growth or to its weakness and decline.

To worship in prayer, song, and Bible study, we should also take practical steps. When we come to hear the Word of God, it is attention with intention. So we should come with an attitude that says, "What does God want to say to me today?" You should bring your Bible and something to take notes with. Leave your cell phone in your car (or at least turn it off). Don't talk to people during worship or the message. Don't arrive late or leave early. Let's follow the steadfast example of the early believers.

4 The Joys of Serving and Giving

Worship is giving God the best that
He has given you. —Oswald Chambers

I have always been a bit of a prankster. I like to have fun.
So when I was a kid, on more than one occasion I heard
someone say, "Will you grow up?" It was their way of saying
I was too much of a goof-off or that I was behaving like a
child, and of course they were usually right.

It seems to me that some people grow up before their
time. They are so responsible, so mature, so dependable,
and by the
age of five, they are telling all the other kids what to do.

But my philosophy is that you might as well enjoy your
childhood, because you have to grow up soon enough.
Often we don't fully appreciate our childhood until much
later in life. Sometimes we wish we could go back to being
a kid again. I once heard someone describe the highlights
of childhood. Here are some of them:

Decisions were made by saying, "Eeney meeney
miney moe."

Mistakes were corrected by simply exclaiming,
"Do over!"

Money issues were handled by whoever was the
banker in Monopoly.

Catching fireflies could happily occupy an entire
evening.

It wasn't odd to have two or three best friends.

Being old referred to anyone over twenty.

The net on a tennis court was the perfect height to play volleyball … and rules didn't matter.

Nobody was prettier than Mom.

Scrapes and bruises were made better by kisses.

Baseball cards in the spokes transformed any bike into a motorcycle.

Water balloons were the ultimate weapon.

Ice cream was considered a basic food group.

How times have changed.

Time to Grow Up

While this may come as a revelation to some, we can't stay children forever. We have to grow up sometime. And that is true of us spiritually as well. Paul spoke of this when he said, "When I was a child, I spoke as a child, I understood as a child, I thought as a child; but when I became a man, I put away childish things" (1 Cor. 13:11).

We all started the Christian life as spiritual babies when we were born again. Some were raised in the church and have always been familiar with the Bible, worship, and other fundamentals of the Christian faith. For others, like me, it was like a completely new world, with a completely new outlook. But the idea is that young believers are to eventually grow up.

Of course, babies are sweet and adorable … and completely selfish. They expect (and often get) the world to cater to their whims. Of course, it is cute for babies to be babies. We are delighted when they smile, laugh, or even burp. And to get children to eat, we often will entertain them: "Here comes the airplane!" we say as we bring the loaded spoon in for a landing. It is one thing to do this with a one-year-old. But it is quite another to have to do this with an eighteen-year-old. We must grow up and not stay like babies forever.

In his first epistle, John addresses believers as "little children," as "young men," and as "fathers." We all have to progress though these stages of spiritual maturity. And we can find a number of traits that are evident in both children and *spiritual* children.

First, children are fickle. A child can go from laughing to crying in a millisecond—sometimes doing both at once. They can go from total happiness to complete misery, or vice versa, in a very brief period of time.

> *To grow means that we must apply ourselves, with discipline, every day.*

Young believers can be that way too. They are often emotionally oriented at first, experiencing a lot of high highs and low lows. They, like children, can change their opinions and views very quickly. That is because they are not totally sure of what they believe. Their ideas are often built on the last preacher they heard or the last book they read. Or, they believe something to be true because they experienced it. In short, they lack a strong foundation. This is understandable for someone who is new in the faith. But as the writer of Hebrews observed, it is sad when this is true of someone who has been a Christian for quite some time:

> You have been Christians a long time now, and you ought to be teaching others. Instead, you need someone to teach you again the basic things a beginner must learn about the Scriptures. You are like babies who drink only milk and cannot eat solid food.

And a person who is living on milk isn't very far along in the Christian life and doesn't know much about doing what is right. (Heb. 5:12–13 NLT)

Second, children don't use any constraint or willpower. When they want something, they want it *now.* If babies are hungry, they just cry. If they want a certain toy, they scream for it. They are impatient and want to advance quickly. They hate to wait for anything.

> *We must learn the joy and blessing of giving to God and others.*

When I first came to Christ, I wanted to know the shortcut to spiritual success. And three years later at age twenty-one, I pretty much felt I had arrived and had most of the answers for most people's questions. It's too bad you didn't know me then. I had a fast answer for every question and an immediate solution for every problem. The truth is, I was spouting truths I had heard others say and had not yet lived them all out in my own life. Today, at the writing of this book, I am 53. Looking back, I realize there is no shortcut to spiritual growth or success. It takes time and discipline. I have written about this at length in my book, *Losers and Winners, Saints and Sinners: How to Finish Strong in the Spiritual Race.*

Third, children like new and exciting things. They might be playing with and thoroughly enjoying their favorite toy when they see a commercial on TV for something new. Suddenly, they have to have *that.* It is all they can talk about, whine about, and pester you about until they get it. Once they get it, they quickly move on to something else.

Unfortunately, many adults are still this way. And young

Christians—or infant-like ones—are this way too. They find novelty very appealing. Acts 17 tells us the people in Athens spent their time "in nothing else but either to tell or to hear some new thing" (v. 21). That is typical of a childlike mentality.

But it is time for us to grow up as believers. To grow means that we must apply ourselves, with discipline, every day. To grow and succeed spiritually requires a combination of not doing some things and actively doing others.

The Fourth Secret

So far, we have learned that to know spiritual success, we must read, study, and love God's Word. We must have a regular and consistent prayer life. We also must be an active part of the church.

And then there is the fourth secret to spiritual success: *We must grow up and learn the joy of giving to and serving others.* In the last chapter, we looked at the powerful effect of the early church on their world. They were spiritually strong, healthy, and vibrant—and they turned their world upside down. Why? Because they were a W. E. L. L. church: a worshipping church, an evangelistic church, a learning church, and a loving church. This was a church that looked out for one another, a church in which everyone did their part. It was a church that was mature.

God is the One who decides what gifts we will have.

We, too, must grow past that phase in our lives in which we are coming to church only to receive. We must learn the joy and blessing of giving to God and others. We may think that happiness and joy come from being served. But the ultimate fulfillment and joy come from serving others. It is also a sign of spiritual maturity. Jesus said, "And whoever of you desires to be first shall be slave of all. For even the Son of Man did not come to be served, but to serve, and to give His life a ransom for many" (Mark 10:44–45). Jesus came not only to save us from our sin, but also to make us like himself. Philippians 2:5–7 tells us, "Your attitude should be the same as that of Christ Jesus: Who, being in very nature God, did not consider equality with God something to be grasped, but made himself nothing, taking the very nature of a servant, being made in human likeness" (NIV). Therefore, we should be serving the Lord.

Ironically, it is often young believers who are more than willing to serve, while those who are older and more mature in the faith don't want to. I have found that those who know the least often want to serve the most, and those who know the most usually want to serve the least. That is sad and wrong.

It is a choice we make to serve.

New believers often are filled with passionate zeal for Christ, because they are still in the first bloom of their new relationship with Jesus. But they lack a good foundation and need to mature and grow in their knowledge of God and His Word. In contrast, there are believers who have known the Lord and have been studying His Word for years, yet they have lost much of that first-love passion that the new believers possess. We need to recognize that just as important as input is in our Christian lives, output is required as well. God's blessings and truths are not given to be hoarded, but to share with others. We have been blessed to be a blessing to others. But it is a choice we make to serve.

Joshua made that choice. He told the people of Israel, "But if serving the Lord seems undesirable to you, then choose for yourselves this day whom you will serve, whether the gods your forefathers served beyond the River, or the gods of the Amorites, in whose land you are living. But as for me and my household,
we will serve the Lord" (Josh. 24:15 NIV).

The fact is that serving the Lord is a true test of who is really right with God and who is not. As Malachi 3:18 says, "And you will again see the distinction between the righteous and the wicked, between those who serve God and those who do not" (NIV).

We All Have a Part to Play

So how do we serve the Lord? *First, we serve Him by finding and using our spiritual gifts.* In the Book of Ephesians, Paul compares the church to a body in which everyone is doing his or her part:

> That we should no longer be children, tossed to and
> fro and carried about with every wind of doctrine,
> by the trickery of men, in the cunning craftiness of
> deceitful plotting, but, speaking the truth in love,
> may grow up in all things into Him who is the head—
> Christ—from whom the whole body, joined and knit
> together by what every joint supplies, according to
> the effective working by which every part does its
> share, causes growth of the body for the edifying
> of itself in love. (Eph. 4:14–16)

Each part of the body is important. And our service, our involvement in the church, is an outgrowth of our worship.

God wants to give us spiritual gifts. Ephesians 4:7–8 says, "But to each one of us grace was given according to the measure of Christ's gift. Therefore He says: 'When He ascended on high, He led captivity captive, and gave gifts to men.'" And God is the One who decides what gifts we will have, as Romans 12:5–6 tells us: "So we, being many, are one body in Christ, and individually members of one another. Having then *gifts differing according to the grace* that is given to us, *let us use them …*" (emphasis mine). These gifts God gives us have nothing to do with any merit on our part; they are given by God as a result of His grace. Paul identified some of these spiritual gifts in Romans 12:

> God has given each of us the ability to do certain things well. So if God has given you the ability to prophesy, speak out when you have faith that God is speaking through you. If your gift is that of serving others, serve them well. If you are a teacher, do a good job of teaching. If your gift is to encourage others, do it! If you have money, share it generously. If God has given you leadership ability, take the responsibility seriously. And if you have a gift for showing kindness to others, do it gladly.
> (vv. 6–8 NLT)

We can discover what gifts we have been given simply by going out and serving. Volunteer for whatever area in your church needs help, and you may find out what your gifts are simply through the process of elimination. You may realize that you are gifted in speaking, teaching, and leading others to Christ. (One of the best places to discover this is by teaching children.) Then again, God may have given you administrative gifts. Whatever your gift may be, just engage, because every part of the body is important and "causes growth of the body for the edifying of itself in love" (Eph. 4:16). So we see from these verses that we need to love and serve others.

Second, we serve Him by learning how to give. Many believers haven't learned how to do this yet. Or at least, they may have heard about the importance of giving, but they just don't want to do it. It reminds me of the man who went to church with his family, and as they drove home afterward, he began complaining about everything. He said, "The music was too loud, the sermon was too long, the announcements were unclear, the building was hot, and the people were unfriendly." He went on and on.

Finally, his son, who was very observant, said, "Dad, you've got to admit that it wasn't a bad show just for a dollar."

Sadly, some of us give more to a waitress as a tip after a meal than we give to the Lord, who has saved our very souls.

> The Bible tells us there can be great joy in giving.

The Blessing of Giving

Many of us don't like to think about giving to God. In fact, the very mention of the subject of money and giving makes us uncomfortable, especially when it comes to the prospect of parting with any of it. However, the Bible tells us there can be great joy in giving.

Have you discovered that joy yet? Jesus said, " 'It is more blessed to give than to receive' " (Acts 20:35). The word "blessed" means "happy." So if you want to be a happy person, then be a generous person.

Money is such an important topic in the Bible that it is the main subject of nearly half the parables Jesus told. In addition, one of every seven verses in the New Testament deals with the topic. To give you an idea of how this compares with other subjects, Scripture offers about five hundred verses on prayer, fewer than five hundred on faith, and more than two thousand verses on the subject of money. Maybe that is because, as Jesus said, "Where your treasure is, there your heart will be also" (Matt. 5:20).

To be successful Christians means that God will have control in every area of our lives. No one is following Jesus completely if they have not learned how to give. And as Martin Luther said, "There are three conversions necessary: the conversion of the heart, mind, and the purse."

When General Sam Houston gave his life to Christ in his later years and was preparing to be baptized, he was reminded to remove any valuables before being immersed in the water. He took off his glasses, removed some papers from his vest pocket, and handed over his watch. The pastor who was about to baptize him noticed that Houston still had his wallet in his back pocket and asked if he wanted to remove that as well.

"If there is any part of me that needs baptizing, it is my wallet!" Houston replied. So he went in, wallet and all.

Has your wallet been "baptized" yet? Let's see what the Bible says about discovering (or rediscovering) the joy of giving:

> But this I say: He who sows sparingly will also reap sparingly, and he who sows bountifully will also reap bountifully. So let each one give as he purposes in his heart, not grudgingly or of necessity; for God loves a cheerful giver. And God is able to make all grace

abound toward you, that you, always having all suffi-
ciency in all things, may have an abundance for every
good work. (2 Cor. 9:6–8)

First we see from this passage that our motive is very
important: "for God loves a cheerful giver" (v. 7). Or as
another translation reads, "For God loves the person who
gives cheerfully" (NLT). The word used here for "cheerful"
also could be translated, "hilarious." This suggests a certain
joy in giving that leaps over all restraints. The Macedonian
Christians understood the absolute joy of giving. In speaking of them to the believers at Corinth, Paul said, "Though
they have been going through much trouble and hard times,
their wonderful joy and deep poverty have overflowed in
rich generosity" (2 Cor. 8:2 NLT). How is it that the phrases
"much trouble," "hard times," "deep poverty," and "rich
generosity," all fit together in one verse? It is because giving
is not only a luxury reserved for the wealthy. It is also a
privilege of the poor—and everyone for that matter. Studies
have shown that those who make the least give the most,
while those who make the most give the least.

*If you want to be a happy person,
then be a generous person.*

So what was the secret of the Macedonian Christians?
We find it in 2 Corinthians 8:5: "They first gave themselves to the Lord, and then to us by the will of God." In
the same way, if we give ourselves to God, then we also will
give of our money. God can have our money and not have
our hearts, but He cannot have our hearts and not have our
money. In fact, the believers in Macedonia were so blessed
by giving that they wanted to do more. Paul wrote, "They

begged us again and again for the gracious privilege of sharing in the gift for the Christians in Jerusalem" (2 Cor. 8:4 NLT). Paul didn't beg them; rather, they begged him! How often do you hear of someone begging to give? These first-century Christians had discovered the joy of giving.

The same was true of the Israelites when the tabernacle was being built:

> And they spoke to Moses, saying, "The people bring much more than enough for the service of the work which the Lord commanded us to do." So Moses gave a commandment, and they caused it to be proclaimed throughout the camp, saying, "Let neither man nor woman do any more work for the offering of the sanctuary." And the people were restrained from bringing, for the material they had was sufficient for all the work to be done—indeed too much. (Ex. 36:5–7)

They were so caught up in the excitement that they had to be restrained from giving, because they had already given beyond what was needed.

> *If we give ourselves to God, then we also will give of our money.*

The next thing we see from 2 Corinthians 9:6–8 is that as we give, God will give to us: "And God will generously provide all you need. Then you will always have everything you need and plenty left over to share with others" (NLT). These are two incredible promises for the believer. God is promising that if we have the right attitude and are generous, that He will bless us. So in reality, if our financial condition is bad, it could be because, in a sense, we have reaped what we have sown: "He who sows sparingly will also reap sparingly, and he who sows bountifully will also reap bountifully" (v. 6). As one commentator said,

> With what confidence can we ask the Lord for more substance if we have not honored Him with the substance we've already been given? What we withhold withers, but what we scatter, gathers. What we lay aside spoils, but what we release, returns. If we fulfill another's needs, God will fill our needs!

This was the truth Jesus was conveying when He said, "Give, and it will be given to you. A good measure, pressed down, shaken together and running over, will be poured into your lap. For with the measure you use, it will be measured to you" (Luke 6:38 NIV).

Some people say they can't afford to give. I can't afford *not to*. David said he would not give the Lord that which cost him nothing (see 2 Sam. 24:24; 1 Chron. 21:24). Someone may say, "If I had a million dollars, then I would give more to the Lord." But that is not necessarily true. The person who has a million dollars could say, "If I had ten million dollars, then I would give more to the Lord." It is all relative.

A preacher asked a farmer in his congregation, "If you had two hundred dollars, would you give one hundred of them to the Lord?"

"I would," the farmer said.

"If you had two cows, would you give one of them to the Lord?"

"I would," the farmer said again.

The preacher then asked, "If you had two pigs, would you give one of them to the Lord?"

"Now that isn't fair," said the farmer. "You know I have two pigs!"

God is saying that as we give to Him, He will give even more to us. But let's not misunderstand. This is not some kind of bargain we strike with God that requires Him to multiply backto us what we give to Him. That would be giving to get something in return, and God will not honor this, because we are giving with an improper motive. We should not fall into the trap of "giving to get," but we should instead give to receive, because God has so graciously given to us.

Our Guidelines for Giving

I want to close this chapter with some very practical words on the subject of giving:

> Now about the money being collected for the Christians in Jerusalem: You should follow the same procedures I gave to the churches in Galatia. On every Lord's Day, each of you should put aside some amount of money in relation to what you have earned and save it for this offering. Don't wait until I get there and then try to collect it all at once. When I come I will write letters of recommendation for the messengers you choose to deliver your gift to Jerusalem. (1 Cor. 16:1–3 NLT)

These were specific instructions Paul was giving to the believers in Corinth. From these verses and from what we read in Philippians and other passages, we can see that Paul addressed the subject of money and giving a number of times. He was not afraid or ashamed to talk about it, nor was it something he harped on. But he did deal with it.

Many people are paranoid about this subject, partially

because of some abuse in this area. But those who are uncomfortable hearing about it are usually the ones who are not giving. The true disciple of Jesus is always interested in what the Bible says, regardless of the subject. So what do we learn about giving from these verses?

*Giving is an essential
part of the Christian life.*

1. Every believer in every church should give. "You should follow the same procedures I gave to the churches in Galatia" (v. 1 NLT). This was to be a universal practice. It was not something only the Corinthians were asked to do. Everywhere Paul went, wherever he founded a church, he taught believers how to give, because giving is an essential part of the Christian life.

2. It is to be done every week. "On every Lord's Day, each of you should put aside some amount of money in relation to what you have earned and save it for this offering" (v. 2 NLT). This is one of the first indications we have in the Epistles that, by this time, the Christians had begun to gather regularly to worship, pray, and give on Sunday, the first day of the week. The Jewish day of worship was on Saturday (actually beginning Friday evening), so we see these first-century Christians had abandoned that and began to worship on Sunday, the first day of the week and the day of the Resurrection.

3. Giving is a personal act. "Each of you should put aside some amount of money … " (v. 2 NLT). Paul didn't leave anyone out. Even children should be taught to give. It may be only a few pennies, a nickel, or a dime they put in the offering, but on every Sunday, there ought to be a gift from every Christian. When I was in military school as a young boy, I was given ten cents to put in the offering during the chapel service. I decided to keep it for the canteen later that week. I didn't end up enjoying the candy I bought with that money. I felt guilty, because even then I knew that money had been set apart for God, not me.

We should set apart money for the work of the kingdom out of every paycheck. After all, we set aside money for taxes and expenses. We should do the same for the Lord's work. Some may argue that this is legalism. But is it? Is it legalistic to say a prayer of thanks before a meal or to set Sunday apart as the Lord's Day? Is it legalistic to discipline yourself to read the Bible on a regular basis? To do these things is not legalism; it is simply good planning and obedience.

4. Giving is a forethought; not an afterthought. "Each of you should put aside some amount of money in relation to what you have earned and save it for this offering. Don't wait until I get there and then try to collect it all at once" (v. 2 NLT). This means that you are ready and prepared when the offering comes, rather than fumbling around with your wallet or checkbook as though the offering were some kind of surprise. It means you have come to church ready to give as an act of worship.

Giving, serving, worshipping, praying, and studying … these are disciplines of the Christian life. If you want to be a successful Christian, then these must be part of your life every day. And there is one more discipline I want to share with you, so read on.

5 Passing **It On**

*We should not ask, "What is wrong with the world?"
for that diagnosis has already been given. Rather,
we should ask, "What has happened to the salt
and light?"* —John R. W. Stott

Y ears ago, my wife Cathe and I took our oldest son
Christopher to Disneyland, where we decided to take
in one of the parades. At that time, the animated film, *The
Rescuers*, had just been released, and one of the characters
from the film would be making a much-anticipated appearance. Suddenly, there he was at the end of Main Street.
Everyone began applauding and cheering as he came
running down the parade route. As I was watching this
giant bird (or should I say a man in a giant bird costume)
coming closer and closer, I noticed that he seemed to be
headed rather quickly in my direction. So I stepped back a
little, but he still seemed to be coming straight toward me.
And sure enough, when he arrived at where we were standing, he came up and threw his giant bird wings around me.
Everyone was staring at me. I was feeling kind of foolish.
Then from inside the costume, I heard a voice say, "Praise
the Lord, Pastor Greg!" It turned out to be someone who
went to Harvest Christian Fellowship. Meanwhile, he was
still holding on, and everyone was still staring.

"Hey, listen," he said. "Do you want to come and meet
some of the other characters afterwards?"

"Uh, OK. That would be good," I said.

"Great!"

So after the parade, Cathe and I took Christopher, who was very young at the time, over to the cast members' area. As we were standing there with all the characters, our host reached up and took off the head of his costume—the giant bird head. All of the sudden, I glanced over at Christopher, who was standing there wide-eyed, taking it all in. This giant bird had just removed his head, and in its place was a little human head. It got even more bizarre when Donald Duck and other familiar animated characters removed their heads. I think Christopher still breaks out in a cold sweat whenever he sees a Disney character. I may have traumatized him for life over our little behind-the-scenes visit.

We have been given a commission to lead others to Christ and then disciple them.

When you have a child, you begin to see things through a child's eyes again. As they discover things for the first time, it helps us as parents to rediscover the newness of things. It is wonderful when, for the first time, a child discovers the chill of the ocean, or walks on the warm sand, or picks up fresh-fallen snow, or tastes cold ice cream. These are things we often take for granted as adults. But when we see children discover them, we share in their excitement.

In the same way, when we see a new believer discover things from God's Word and the excitement it brings, it reignites us. Often they will ask difficult questions that have us searching the Scriptures for answers. Then there are things we have learned, but sometimes have since forgotten.

As followers of Jesus, we have been given a commission to lead others to Christ and then disciple them: "Go therefore and make disciples of all the nations, baptizing them in the name of the Father and of the Son and of the Holy Spirit, teaching them to observe all things that I have commanded you; and lo, I am with you always, even to the end of the age" (Matt. 28:19–20).

The Fifth Secret

We have been talking about the secrets of spiritual success, disciplines that every believer must constantly have in play in their lives: we must we must read, study, and love God's Word. We must have a regular and consistent prayer life. We must be an active part of the church. We must grow up and learn the joy of giving to and serving others.

And last, we must actively look for opportunities to share the gospel and disciple others. We have focused a lot on the importance of Bible study, prayer, and other things we need to do to grow. But it is possible to overeat, so to speak. It is not good to simply sit in the pew and absorb truth. We also need an outlet for the truth we are discovering. As already stated, we have been blessed in order to be a blessing to others. Input without output can be hazardous to our spiritual growth. Jesus said, "For whoever has, to him more will be given, and he will have abundance; but whoever does not have, even what he has will be taken away from him" (Matt. 13:12). It comes down to this: evangelize or fossilize.

I have found that the more I give, the more God gives back to me. Proverbs 11:25 tells us, "The generous soul will be made rich, and he who waters will also be watered himself." As we "water," or give out to others, God will give back to us. We need to take what God has given us and use it constructively in the lives of others. Often when you take a new believer under your wing, you are not only saving a sinner from hell, but you are saving yourself from spiritual stagnation. James 5:19 says, "Brethren, if anyone among you wanders from the truth, and someone turns him back, let him know that he who turns a sinner from the error of his way will save a soul from death and cover a multitude of sins." We need the zeal, spark, and childlike simplicity of faith that new believers possess.

Have you ever led anyone to Jesus Christ? Have you discipled anyone? Have you taken a new believer under your wing and helped him or her along? If we really believe what we claim to believe, then we must tell others. Do we really believe there is a heaven and hell and that the wages of sin are death? If so, then how can we be so casual about telling others?

The Sermon that Started it All

A survey taken among Christians revealed that 95 percent had never led another person to Jesus Christ. Personal salvation should be the number-one concern for our children, parents, family, and friends. If you want to be a strong and successful Christian, then you must share the gospel. And I want to encourage you and help you to see that God can indeed use you to bring others into His kingdom.

Maybe you have already tried to do this, but you have failed. It could be that you are simply missing some basics that you need to know. There may be some key ingredients missing in your presentation of the gospel, which means that the gospel you are proclaiming may not technically be the gospel. It would be like baking a chocolate cake and forgetting the sugar, or the flour, or worse yet, the chocolate.

So, what are these key ingredients necessary for the gospel to be the gospel? We find them in the story before us. We have been looking at the effectiveness of the early church. So now let's look at the sermon that set the church in motion. Although it is some two thousand years old, it is a classic prototype for effectively bringing the gospel to our culture. In spite of our amazing advances in technology, the basic needs of humanity have not changed—even slightly— from the first century to the twenty-first century. Nor has the solution to our problems.

We have been blessed in order to be a blessing to others.

Aside from the messages of Jesus, this is one of the greatest sermons ever preached. It is great because of the place it occupies in the history of redemption. This was the church's inaugural sermon. It is also great because of the number of people who responded to it: some three thousand in all. And it is great because it is essentially a model for effective evangelism.

It is pretty amazing to consider the fact that some fifty days earlier, the man who gave this message, Simon Peter, had radically denied the Lord. Sometimes we don't realize how dramatic that denial was. But Peter was recommissioned by Jesus and empowered by the Holy Spirit, who had been poured out on this great gathering of people. So Peter seized the moment to boldly proclaim the gospel message:

> "Men of Israel, hear these words: Jesus of Nazareth, a Man attested by God to you by miracles, wonders, and signs which God did through Him in your midst, as you yourselves also know—Him, being delivered by the determined purpose and foreknowledge of God, you have taken by lawless hands, have crucified, and put to death; whom God raised up, having loosed

the pains of death, because it was not possible that
He should be held by it." (Acts 2:22–24)

Peter went on to show how Jesus Christ was the long-
awaited Messiah of Israel, fulfilling many Old Testament
prophecies. Then, he wrapped it up, commanding a
response to the truth he proclaimed:

> "Therefore let all the house of Israel know assuredly
> that God has made this Jesus, whom you crucified,
> both Lord and Christ." Now when they heard this,
> they were cut to the heart, and said to Peter and the
> rest of the apostles, "Men and brethren, what shall we
> do?" Then Peter said to them, "Repent, and let every
> one of you be baptized in the name of Jesus Christ for
> the remission of sins; and you shall receive the gift of
> the Holy Spirit. For the promise is to you and to your
> children, and to all who are afar off, as many as the
> Lord our God will call." And with many other words
> he testified and exhorted them, saying, "Be saved
> from this perverse generation." (vv. 36–40)

*Input without output can be
hazardous to our spiritual growth.*

Now let's consider what made this message remarkable,
and what made it such an effective gospel presentation. For
in doing so, we can unlock some vital principles for our own
efforts in sharing the Lord with others.

First, Peter's message was scriptural. He quoted Joel
2:28–32 (see v. 28), apparently from memory. A few verses
later, we see that he quoted from Psalm 16 and Psalm 110.
Obviously, Peter had committed great portions of Scripture

to memory. And every Christian who wants to be successful spiritually should be able to stand up, on a moment's notice, and clearly articulate the gospel message without notes. I cannot emphasize enough the importance of quoting Scripture when you share the gospel. That is why Paul encouraged Timothy to "be a good worker, one who does not need to be ashamed and who correctly explains the word of truth" (2 Tim. 2:15 NLT).

It comes down to this: evangelize or fossilize.

And the man who preached this very message told us to do the same in his epistle: "Always be prepared to give an answer to everyone who asks you to give the reason for the hope that you have. But do this with gentleness and respect" (1 Pet. 3:15 NIV). The phrase "give an answer" is from the Greek word *apologia*, which means a legal defense, as in a court of law.

When it comes to sharing our faith, nothing is more effective than quoting the Bible. And God, speaking through the prophet Isaiah, gives us this promise:

> "For as the rain comes down, and the snow from heaven, and do not return there, but water the earth, and make it bring forth and bud, that it may give seed to the sower and bread to the eater, so shall My word be that goes forth from My mouth; it shall not return to Me void, but it shall accomplish what I please, and it shall prosper in the thing for which I sent it." (Isa. 55:10–11)

As we share our faith with others, we must know God's Word, just as artists would know their brushes, pens, or computer software; just as builders would know their tools, and just as ancient soldiers would know their swords. This is because God's Word simply will not return without effect.

I heard about a man who took his wife to see the doctor. The doctor told him to stay in the waiting room, and he would be called when the doctor had finished examining his wife. After a little while, the doctor came out of the exam room and asked the nurse for a screwdriver. Then he went back into the room. A few minutes later, the doctor reappeared and asked for a pair of pliers, then once again returned to the room. When the doctor emerged from the room and asked for a hammer, the man could not contain himself any longer.

"Doctor, what is wrong with my wife?" he asked.

"I don't know yet," the doctor replied. "I can't get my medical bag open."

> *We need to take what God has given us and use it constructively in the lives of others.*

We'd better make sure we get our Bibles open and use the Word of God. Ephesians 6 mentions the only offensive weapon in our spiritual arsenal, "the sword of the Spirit, which is the word of God" (v. 17). The devil knows all too well the power and authority of the Bible, even if we don't. And He will try to keep us from it at all costs. He will do everything he can to see that we either keep our swords sheathed or that we don't put them on in the first place.

What shape is your sword in? Is it polished from daily use as you study the Bible on a regular basis? Is it sharpened on the anvil of experience as you have applied and obeyed its truth in your life? Or, is it rusty from lack of preparation or dulled by disobedience?

Even if the person we are speaking to doesn't believe the Bible, we should still quote it. After all, if you were going into battle against someone who did not believe your sword was sharp, would that change anything? No. Once you began using your sword effectively, they would know it was sharp. The same is true of God's Word. When it goes out, it doesn't return without accomplishing what God intends it to.

Conversion is the work of God and God alone.

Second, Peter's message was remarkable, because it was Christ-centered. Notice the phrases he used: "Jesus of Nazareth" (v. 22); "This Jesus God has raised up" (v. 32); and "God has made this Jesus, whom you crucified, both Lord and Christ" (v. 36). Peter spoke of the crucifixion and resurrection of Jesus Christ. And this cannot be emphasized enough. Whatever springboard you choose to employ, it should always come back to Jesus and His death on the cross. Paul said, "For since, in the wisdom of God, the world through wisdom did not know God, it pleased God through the foolishness of the message preached to save those who believe. For Jews request a sign, and Greeks seek after wisdom; but we preach Christ crucified … " (1 Cor. 1:21–23). Again, he emphasized this essential message a few verses later: "For I determined not to know anything among you except Jesus Christ and Him crucified" (1 Cor. 2:2). In his epistle to the Romans, Paul wrote, "For I am not ashamed of the gospel of Christ, for *it is the power of God* to salvation for everyone who believes, for the Jew first and also for the Greek" (Rom. 1:16, emphasis mine). Paul had the right idea.

We often underestimate the raw power the gospel has in reaching even the most hardened heart. Don't underestimate its appeal. Don't be embarrassed by its simplicity. Don't add to it or take away from it. Just proclaim it, and stand back and watch what God will do.

Paul also warned against diluting the message of the gospel, saying that God had called him to preach the gospel "not with wisdom of words, lest the cross of Christ should be made of no effect" (1 Cor. 1:17), or literally, "deprived of its power."

Maybe we have thought that if we could only perform miracles, then people would believe us. The Pharisees came to Jesus, demanding a sign from Him. This was in spite of the fact that He had performed many signs already. Among many things, he had restored hearing to the deaf, sight to the blind, and had raised a man from the dead. Jesus told them, "A wicked and adulterous generation seeks after a sign, and no sign shall be given to it except the sign of the prophet Jonah" (Matt. 16:4). He was saying, in other words, "This is my sign to you. Take it or leave it." He knew they would leave it, because they had no intention of believing him in the first place.

> I cannot emphasize enough the importance of quoting Scripture when you share the gospel.

The same is true of our culture today. Ten million signs and wonders would not make this world turn to Christ, because belief is a choice—an act of the will. And the message we are to preach is Christ and Him crucified.

I once asked Billy Graham if he had it to do all over again, what he would emphasize more now that he may not have emphasized as a younger preacher. Without hesitation, he replied, "The cross and the blood of Christ. That's where the power is."

So, what is this essential message we call the gospel? And what are the elements that must be present for the gospel to be the gospel? A technical definition of the gospel is "good news." We have all heard the expression, "I have some good news and some bad news. … " Upon hearing that statement, we usually expect the worst, like the patient whose doctor told him, "I have some good news and bad news."

"What is the good news?" the patient asked.

"You have only three weeks to live," the doctor said.

"If that is the good news, then what is the bad news?"

"Well," said the doctor. "I found out two weeks ago, and I forgot to tell you."

Unless people understand the bad news about sin and judgment, how can they appreciate the good news about God's love and forgiveness in Jesus Christ? We make a grave mistake when we present Jesus as a mere additive to one's life that will deliver happiness and a more successful life. Jesus is not one of many roads to follow. In fact, it is frightening how many Christians today hold the view that says, "Whatever a person wants to believe is okay, as long as they are sincere and mean well." Some well-meaning, but misled, believers might say, "Jesus is the best way, and it's the way I have personally chosen, but there are other ways to God besides Christ." That is simply wrong. We may justify ourselves by feeling we are simply being loving, but in reality, the most unloving thing we could do for a person is to mislead him or her. And that is exactly what we are doing if we do not take the biblical position that Jesus Christ is the only way to a relationship with God.

The reason I believe Jesus Christ is the only way to God the Father is because He said of himself, "I am the way, the truth, and the life. No one comes to the Father except through Me" (John 14:6). Also, we are told in Acts 4:12, "Salvation is found in no one else, for there is no other name under heaven given to men by which we must be saved" (NIV). And 1 Timothy 2:5 says, "For there is only one God and one Mediator who can reconcile God and people. He is the man Christ Jesus" (NLT). If we declare anything less, then it is a false gospel, as Galatians warns:

> I am astonished that you are so quickly deserting the one who called you by the grace of Christ and are turning to a different gospel—which is really no gospel at all. Evidently some people are throwing you into confusion and are trying to pervert the gospel of Christ. But even if we or an angel from heaven should preach a gospel other than the one we preached to you, let him be eternally condemned! (Gal. 1:6–8 NIV)

The devil knows all too well the power and authority of the Bible, even if we don't.

The bad news, as we have already seen, is the fact that we all stand as sinners before a holy God. We have offended God and have willfully broken His commandments. When the rich young ruler came to Jesus and asked what he must do to find eternal life, Jesus pointed him to God's commandments (see Mark 10:17–22). Did Jesus do this because a person is saved by keeping them? No. It is because God's commandments awaken us to our sinful condition. Romans 3:19 says, "Now we know that whatever the law says, it says to those who are under the law, so that every mouth may be silenced and the whole world held accountable to God" (NIV). No matter who we are, we all have sinned, sometimes in ignorance and often on purpose.

So upon seeing our complete weakness and inability to do anything whatsoever to alleviate our wretched condition, God did the ultimate for us:

> For when we were still without strength, in due time Christ died for the ungodly. For scarcely for a righteous man will one die; yet perhaps for a good man someone would even dare to die. But God demonstrates His own love toward us, in that while we were still sinners, Christ died for us. (Rom. 5:6–7)

Because there was no other way to satisfy the righteous demands of God, because of our inability to improve ourselves, much less save ourselves, because we faced a future in hell because of our sin, Christ died for us.

So, coming back to Peter's message, how did the people respond that day? The Bible tells us "they were cut to the heart" (v. 37). That is the only place this phrase appears in the New Testament. The word "cut" means "to pierce" or "to stab," and thus depicts something sudden and unexpected. So it is with the conviction of the Holy Spirit. John 16:8 tells us, "And when He has come, He will *convict the world of sin*, and of righteousness, and of judgment … " (emphasis mine). It suddenly dawned on Peter's audience that they had been responsible for the very death of their long-awaited Messiah, the One for whom they had longed for centuries, the One who was the hope of their nation and their own lives. He had finally come. Instead of welcoming Him, however, they rejected Him and handed him over to the Romans, their bitter and hated enemies, for execution.

Ten million signs and wonders would not make this world turn to Christ, because belief is a choice.

Many of those listening to Peter's message that day had personally played a part in the crucifixion of Christ. It would have been bad enough to learn that the Messiah had been killed. But then to realize they had a hand in it was too much to bear. Overwhelmed with guilt and remorse, they cried out, "What shall we do?" (v. 37).

So Peter gave them (and us) the answer: "Repent, and let every one of you be baptized in the name of Jesus Christ for the remission of sins; and you shall receive the gift of the Holy Spirit. For the promise is to you and to your children, and to all who are afar off, as many as the Lord our God will call" (vv. 38–39). "Repent!" Peter said, and that brings me to another facet of his sermon that I want to point out.

Third, Peter's message was remarkable because he preached repentance. This is a word we rarely hear in most presentations of the gospel today. But it is, in reality, part and parcel of true gospel preaching. If we don't tell people they need to repent, then we have not given them the complete gospel. There are many people who feel remorse for their sin, but never truly repent. Remorse is being sorry. But repentance is being sorry enough to stop. As 2 Corinthians 7:10 reminds us, "Godly sorrow brings repentance that leads to salvation and leaves no regret, but worldly sorrow brings death" (NIV). Phony repentance is like crying when you chop an onion. The eyes produce tears because they are irritated, not because the heart is broken. Repentance means a change of mind and a confession that you were wrong. It means to turn around, to change direction, and to change both the mind and the will.

Repentance does not mean making just any change, but a change from wrong to right, from sin to righteousness.

So if you have shared the whole gospel, have liberally quoted Scripture, have pointed to Jesus Christ as the only way to God, and have emphasized the need to repent, what do you do next? Right then and there, ask whether they want to accept Jesus Christ. I often review the following points when I am bringing a message to a close, and you might want to do the same as you share the gospel:

1. Realize you are a sinner.

2. Recognize Christ died on the cross for your sin.

3. Repent.

4. Receive Jesus Christ into your life.

5. Do it now!

Then, if they agree, lead them in a prayer to make a commitment to Jesus Christ.

> *No matter who we are, we all have sinned,*
> *sometimes in ignorance and often on purpose.*

Some people are critical of evangelistic invitations and keeping track of how many responses there were. This means that Peter would fall under their scrutiny as well, because he challenged those listening to his message to come to Christ. And the Bible tells us that three thousand people responded: "Then those who gladly received his word were baptized; and that day about three thousand souls were added to them" (Acts 2:41).

The results are in God's hands. Jesus said, "Therefore pray the Lord of the harvest to send out laborers into His harvest" (Matt. 9:38). Notice Jesus said, "His harvest," not ours. Conversion is the work of God and God alone. Yes, God uses us to get His message out, but we must be completely dependent upon Him for the results. After all, when Paul preached on Mars Hill, only a handful of people believed (see Acts 17). So we must focus on proclaiming our message accurately and then leave the rest to God.

If God graciously allows us to lead others to Him, then we have the privilege of seeing them grow in their faith as we personally disciple them. Yet we all feel inadequate for this task. Imagine how the disciples must have felt when Jesus told them to go and make disciples of all the nations. "How will we do this?" they might have wondered. They had not only failed in their public witness, but in their private faith as well. Peter, their acknowledged leader, had openly denied the Lord. Yet here he was now, boldly preaching the gospel.

Remorse is being sorry.
But repentance is being sorry enough to stop.

How did he do it? He was like you and me, weak in and of himself. So what brought about the change? It was through a power He hadn't known previously: "But you shall receive power when the Holy Spirit has come upon you; and you shall be witnesses to Me in Jerusalem, and in all Judea and Samaria, and to the end of the earth" (Acts 1:8). Jesus promised the disciples a special power to fulfill the Great Commission. The Holy Spirit was already in them, but He was not yet upon them. What followed was recorded for us in Acts 2 and is known as the Day of Pentecost. And Acts 2:39 tells us that this promise of the Holy Spirit's empowering is also for us today: "For the promise is to you and to your children, and to all who are afar off, as many as the Lord our God will call."

Power is an exciting thing. When you have a fast car, you want it to go even faster—more power. When you're weight training, you want to be even stronger—more power. But God's power is not given to us so that we can be like a fire hose that has been dropped and is wildly spraying in every direction imaginable. God's power is a directed power. It is power with purpose. It is practical power. The word "power" Jesus used in Acts 1:8 originates from the Greek word *dunamis*, the same word from which we get our English word "dynamite." So Jesus was saying, "You shall receive dynamite power when the Holy Spirit has come upon you. … You shall receive power to be a witness, power to share your faith, power to speak up and be counted—and power to turn your world upside down."

Will you pray right now and ask God to give you that power? To be successful Christians, we will need to study the Bible and pray more. We will need to worship and hear God's Word more. We will need to serve and give. And we will need to share our faith. But we are weak. Yet He is strong. And He has the power for us to live the lives He has called us to. He has the power that will help us succeed spiritually. All we need to do is ask.

I know I have not shared anything new or revolutionary in these pages. Sometimes we are so busy looking for new or hidden truth that we miss the obvious. I guarantee that if you will get the disciplines outlined in these chapters working in your life, you will see spiritual change in your life—and ultimately success. I urge you, start today.

May you cross the finish line in the race of life and one day hear our Lord say, "Well done, good and faithful servant. Enter into the joy of your Lord!"

A Final **Word**

I would be making a big mistake if I wrote an entire book on the subject of spiritual success and did not provide an opportunity to take the first and most important step, which is a personal relationship with Jesus Christ.

If you have never asked Christ to come into your life, if you don't have the assurance that you will go to heaven when you die, if you are still carrying a load of guilt around, but you want to be forgiven, if you want to know God in a personal way, then here is what you need to do:

1. *Realize that you are a sinner.* No matter how good of a life we try to live, we still fall miserably short of being a good person. That is because we are all sinners. We all fall short of God's desire for us to be holy. The Bible says, "No one is good—not even one" (Romans 3:10 NLT). This is because we cannot become who we are supposed to be without Jesus Christ.

2. *Recognize that Jesus Christ died on the cross for you.* The Bible tells us, "But God showed His great love for us by sending Christ to die for us while were still sinners" (Romans 5:8 NLT). This is the Good News, that God loves us so much that He sent His only Son to die in our place when we least deserved it.

3. *Repent of your sin.* The Bible tells us to "repent and be converted" (Acts 3:19). The word, "repent," means "to change our direction in life." Instead of running away from God, we can run toward Him.

4. *Receive Jesus Christ into your life.* Becoming
   a Christian is not merely believing some creed
   or going to church on Sunday. It is having Christ
   himself take residence in your life and heart. Jesus
   said, "Behold, I stand at the door [of your life] and
   knock. If anyone hears My voice and opens the
   door, I will come in . . ." (Revelation 3:20).

If you would like to invite Christ into your life, simply
pray a prayer like this one, and mean it in your heart:

*Dear Lord Jesus, I know I am a sinner. I believe you
died for my sins. Right now, I turn from my sins and
open the door of my heart and life. I confess you as
my personal Lord and Savior. Thank you for saving
me. Amen.*

The Bible tells us, "If we confess our sins, he is faithful and just to forgive us our sins and cleanse us from all unrighteousness" (1 John 1:9). If you just prayed that prayer and meant it, then Jesus Christ has now taken residence in your heart! Your decision to follow Christ means God has forgiven you and that you will spend eternity in heaven. It means you will be ready to meet Christ when He returns.

To help you grow in your newfound faith, be sure to make the secrets to spiritual success a part of your life each day by regularly reading the Bible, praying, spending time with other Christians by going to church, and telling others about your faith in Christ.

For additional resources to help you learn more about what it means to be a follower of Jesus Christ, please visit http://www.harvest.org/knowgod/.

About the **Author**

G reg Laurie is the pastor of Harvest Christian Fellowship (one of America's largest churches) in Riverside, California. He is the author of over thirty books, including the Gold Medallion Award winner, *The Upside-Down Church*, as well as *Every Day with Jesus; Are We Living in the Last Days?*; *Marriage Connections; and Losers* and *Winners, Saints and Sinners.* You can find his study notes in the *New Believer's Bible* and the *Seeker's Bible. Host of the Harvest: Greg Laurie* television program and the nationally syndicated radio program, *A New Beginning*, Greg Laurie is also the founder and featured speaker for Harvest Crusades —contemporary, large–scale evange-listic outreaches, which local churches organize nationally and internationally. He and his wife Cathe have two chil-dren and live in Southern California.

Other AllenDavid books
published by Kerygma Publishing

The Great
Compromise

For Every Season:
Daily Devotions

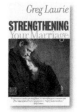

Strengthening
Your Marriage

Marriage
Connections

Are We Living
in the Last Days?

"I'm Going on
a Diet Tomorrow"

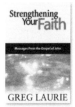

Strengthening
Your Faith

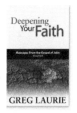

Deepening Your Faith

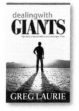

Dealing with Giants

Visit: www.kerygmapublishing.com
www.allendavidbooks.com
www.harvest.org